GARDEN PROBLEM SOLVER

HarperCollins*Publishers (New Zealand) Limited*

First published 1990 as *Yates Garden Doctor*
This edition first published 2000
Reprinted 2000, 2001
HarperCollins*Publishers (New Zealand) Limited*
P.O. Box 1, Auckland

ISBN 1 86950 334 1
Designed and typeset by Graeme Leather
Printed in Hong Kong/China

CONTENTS

INTRODUCTION

Many garden problems can be eliminated or prevented by paying attention to some key factors before you begin planting. Start by examining physical features of the garden that may require alteration to enhance plant growth. Note the soil type, drainage, prevailing winds, amount of sunshine received and where the shade falls. If necessary, modifications should be made to the site before plants are purchased.

Soil provides anchorage for plants and is the medium in which most plants grow and rely on for nutrients and water. Healthy soil promotes healthy plants. Poorly drained soils can be improved by the installation of drainage coils or by altering the soil, building it up with organic materials such as peat and compost. Raised beds filled with good topsoil make an easy, alternative garden. A combination of lime or gypsum plus plentiful helpings of peat and compost will aid in breaking down clay soils, and addition of organic material will help improve sandy soils by increasing water and nutrient retention. Excessively shaded areas may be lightened up by trimming surrounding trees. Hot dry areas may require some planting for shade or an irrigation system (best installed after planting has been completed). If the site is windswept, a shelterbelt will improve the survival chances of more delicate species. Preparation of this sort will help your plants achieve maximum health and avoid disappointing — and costly — losses.

Correct plant selection is paramount to success. There is great wisdom in the often-used quote 'the right plant for the right place'. Plants need to be not only healthy from the outset, but also chosen for their ability to grow in the specified area, so select wind tolerant plants for exposed sites, and moisture tolerant plants for damp soils. Existing plants should be trimmed, fertilised and sprayed as necessary. Cull any which are not thriving or are of an undesirable appearance. Purchase only vigorously growing and healthy new plants, disregarding those that are root bound, show signs of poor nutrition, or harbour pests or disease.

Once the initial hurdles have been overcome and the garden is planted, sound cultural practises will ensure success. Watering, feeding and grooming are considered to be the keys to a healthy garden. Effective water management is one of the most important factors affecting plant growth. Too little water results in wilting and leaf drop, whilst overwatering can cause root rot and, in turn, collapse of the plant.

WATERING

Correct water application is the key to good water management. To make watering easier, arrange your garden so that plants which enjoy similar water requirements are located together. For instance succulents, which enjoy dry conditions, particularly in winter, should be sited away ferns, which like cool moist soil. Localised alteration of the soil can also help achieve desired water levels. Add plenty of compost and humus to soil in which moisture-loving plants are to be grown — this will help keep the soil moist. A layer of mulch — peat, granulated bark or compost — 5–10 cm thick will help conserve water and protect surface roots by reducing evaporation from the soil surface. Mulching also helps to reduce weed infestation, which in turn reduces competition for water and nutrients. Irrigation systems, sprinklers and soaker hoses also aid dramatically in correct water management. Irrigation systems are easy to install and can easily be tailored to suit each part of the garden according to its particular water requirements. Remember, though, that a good soaking every 4–5 days during dry periods is of far more benefit than a quick sprinkle every day. Deep watering encourages roots to grow down, anchoring the plant more effectively, keeping the soil (and the roots) cooler and moister for longer and increasing the plant's nutrient-absorbing efficiency.

FEEDING

Feeding is the second most important factor in promoting a healthy garden. All plants need a particular balance of essential elements. If one is in short supply or unavailable, plant vigour and growth will be reduced. During the growing season, the requirements of plants may change. To maximise growth and ensure your plants are able to withstand pests and disease it is important to feed them regularly. The key elements are listed in the box below.

Most plants require fertilising only in early spring when they are coming into their active growth period. Plants such as annuals and roses, which continue to flower throughout the summer, should also be fertilised in early summer. Plants which flower or fruit in winter benefit from a second application in autumn, as they effectively have two periods of active growth — leaf growth in spring and flower and fruit production in autumn or winter.

GROOMING

Regular grooming of your garden and its plants within will keep you aware of any impending problems, allowing you to halt the spread of pests and diseases before they reach epidemic proportions. Maintaining the garden in a clean and tidy state will prevent many problems. Removal of 'undesirables' such as weeds and senescent plant tissue is the best way to maintain the garden in a healthy state. Weeds not only compete for nutrients and water, they also provide a hiding place for unwanted pests

---

Nitrogen (N)
Essential for protein building, photosynthesis and cell extension, promotes healthy leaf growth.

Phosphorous (P)
Plays an important role in actively dividing plant cells, vital for the healthy development of seedlings, root growth, flowering and the formation of fruit and seeds.

Potassium (K)
Promotes chlorophyll production, which is important for photosynthesis, and plays a vital part in the strengthening of cell walls and movement of water in the plant. It also aids in building the immunity of a plant to pests and disease and improves the quality of fruits, flowers and seeds.

Magnesium (Mg)
Used in the production of chlorophyll.

Sulphur (S)
Forms part of many plant proteins and is used in the production of chlorophyll.

and diseases. Dead or dying plant tissue may also be a source of infection, so is best removed and placed in the rubbish bin. Ensure your pruning equipment is sharp and that the cut tissue does not become infected. Old flowers or fallen leaves left in the garden can harbour fungi, which can in turn infect healthy tissue. Regular pruning aids airflow through and between plants and is particularly important over the humid summer months. Pruning helps control fungal diseases by reducing the humidity necessary for their survival. Applying a copper-based spray, followed a few days later by an oil spray, several times over the winter period, will help control overwintering fungi and insects, reducing the incidence of these the following season. Regular cultivation of the soil betters the conditions for plant growth by improving drainage, bringing nutrients closer to the root zone and aerating the soil. Cultivation also assists weed control, and should be accompanied by mulching, to aid moisture retention.

SPRAYING

In the event of an outbreak of either a pest or a disease, spraying may be the only available option. It should be remembered that once insects or fungi damage a plant, it is not possible to repair that damaged tissue. Spraying will eliminate or control the pest or disease, but it is likely that the plant will also require extra care to ensure the effects are not long lasting. Extra feeding, and/or pruning will aid the plant's recovery. In order to understand the use of crop protection products, we need to know the types available.

Fungicides are for the control of fungal diseases: they fall into two main categories:

- Protectants — a layer of chemicals is deposited on the outside of the plant and prevents fungal spores from germinating.

- Systemic — these enter the plant tissue and stop the growth of the fungi within the plant's cells.

Insecticides are for the control of insects: they also fall into two main categories:

- Contact — these eliminate any insects they come into contact with at the time of spraying.

- Systemic — these enter the plant tissue and will be consumed by the insect in due course.

The type of insecticide necessary depends on the feeding method of the insect. For both insecticides and fungicides, thorough coverage of the plant, including the undersides of the leaves, is important. You can also purchase combination sprays, which contain both an insecticide and a fungicide.

When using sprays, always read the label thoroughly and follow the directions. Ensure you always:

- Identify what you wish to control;

- Read the label to ensure you have the correct product;

- Only make up the amount needed to do the job;

- Follow label directions with regard to precautions, application rate and withholding periods.

There is quite a range of sprays on the market, and many people do not want to keep a lot of chemicals in their garden shed. Some products are useful for controlling a variety of pests and diseases. Yates make the following recommendations:

● SHIELD can be used as a substitute for ORTHENE or FUNGUS FIGHTER

● SUPER SHIELD can be used as a substitute for MAVRIK or FUNGUS FIGHTER

● GARDEN MASTER can be used as a substitute for CARBARYL or MALDISON

ORGANIC CONTROL

If you prefer not to use sprays, there are a few alternatives available. Firstly, not all sprays are composed of synthetic chemicals. There are several effective organic sprays, which are completely safe to use. Bear in mind that these sprays will need to be applied regularly for the most effective control. It is possible to control some insect pests — such as caterpillars and snails — by regularly inspecting plants for infestation and physically picking off insects. Insect traps are another ideal way to control garden pests. It is possible to buy yellow sticky traps, which attract whitefly, and pheromone traps, which attract male codling moths, thereby lessening the population of this pest. Snail houses could be considered garden ornamentation, but are very effective if placed in moist shady areas where slugs and snails enjoy hiding out. Simply empty out the house for the birds once it is full. Not all of the insects in your garden will cause damage to plants. A good many of them — ladybirds, praying mantis, spiders, predatory mites — actually prey on other insects. These insects will help reduce garden pests, and care should be taken that insecticides are not applied indiscriminately as they will also harm these biological helpers. Plants can also be protected by the use of physical barriers — cloches, shade cloth or glasshouses. Whichever protection system is used, it is important that ventilation and moisture levels are adequately controlled. It is also possible to enclose individual fruits in plastic or paper bags to prevent insect damage during ripening.

Lastly, modern plant breeding has resulted in varieties that have been selected for their high yields, improved health and quality, and resistance to pests and disease. Many new and improved plant varieties and hybrid seeds are available to the home gardener through your local garden retailer. As well as choosing high-quality seeds, seedlings and plants, it is wise to have variety in the species you plant. That way you minimise the chance of insects or microbial diseases reaching plague proportions.

SEED GERMINATION

Growing your own seeds from plants can be very cost-effective — providing you get it right! The table below will help you diagnose germination problems.

Soil too wet	Seeds need to be damp, not wet, for germination. Poorly drained soils may also have a high incidence of soil-borne fungal diseases. Wet soil can be improved with the addition of peat or by sowing seed in a band of BLACK MAGIC SEED-RAISING MIX.
Soil too dry	Maintaining a constant level of moisture during the germination period is vital.
Soil too cold	Cold temperatures result in slow, uneven germination; disease becomes prevalent and seedlings may be injured. Each species has a different optimum temperature for germination. Do not sow summer plants too early, e.g. bean, tomato, sweetcorn, pumpkin, melon, cucumber, petunia, portulaca and zinnia.
Planting too deep	This will result in delayed emergence. Seeds may not be able to grow sufficiently to reach the surface on the limited reserve within the seed. Soil temperature is also lower with increasing depth. As a guide, sow seed to a depth equal to twice the thickness of the seed. Very fine flower seed, e.g. begonia and petunia, is best just pressed into the surface.
Planting seeds too shallow	This may cause seeds to dry out.
Seed beds too loose	This results in too much air surrounding the seeds; they will not absorb moisture and are likely to dry out.
Seed beds too firm	This prevents oxygen getting to the seed. Drainage is also impeded.
Presence of soil-borne fungal diseases	Seeds may rot or seedlings topple. Overwatering, poor drainage and lack of ventilation will increase the incidence of these diseases. Sow seeds in sterilised seed-raising mix and ensure containers are clean. Plan a rotation of crops to prevent the build

	up of soil diseases. Sterilising the soil with BASAMID granules will clean up badly diseased soil and should be used in small gardens where crop rotation is difficult. Spray seedlings with CAPTAN at first sign of disease.
Slugs and snails	During the late autumn, winter and spring slugs and snails may destroy seedlings as soon as they appear. Bait areas with BLITZEM every 7–10 days, or with MESUROL every two to three weeks.
Birds, cats, dogs	These are often responsible for destroying seedlings. Cover seed beds with fine-meshed netting.
Insects	Seeds can be damaged or eaten by insects, e.g. springtails, earwigs. Prevent by sowing seed with SOIL INSECT KILLER granules.
Fertiliser burn	Seed in direct contact with fertiliser can be burnt. Fertiliser should be worked into soil several weeks before sowing seed or placed in a band below or beside the seed. Seedlings in the presence of high soluble salts are also more prone to damping-off diseases.
Seed viability and storage	Always use fresh seed. Some seeds, such as parsnip and lettuce, have a short life once the foil packet is opened. Seed deteriorates quickly if stored in a damp place or exposed to high temperatures. Always treat and handle seed with care to prolong its life. As a general guide, once the foil sachet has been opened, the seed should be used within six months.

WEEDS

1   Bamboo
Spray with AMITROLE and SPRAYFIX or ZERO and SPRAYFIX on vigorously growing young foliage, or apply to new spears after cutting off tips.

2   Clover
When in full leaf, spray lawns with WOODY WEED-KILLER and waste areas with AMITROLE.

3   Convolvulus
When in full leaf and actively growing, spray with WOODY WEEDKILLER.

4   Dock
When in full leaf and actively growing, spray with ZERO, AMITROLE or WOODY WEEDKILLER.

5   Fennel
When in full leaf and actively growing, spray with WOODY WEEDKILLER or HYDROCOTYL KILLER, preferably before flowering.

6   Flax
Spray with WOODY WEEDKILLER. Most effective when sprayed on young growth after cutting back. Add SPRAYFIX for improved coverage.

7   Ginger plant
Spray leaves and roots with AMITROLE and SPRAYFIX; may require repeat applications.

8   Gorse
Spray with ZERO and SPRAYFIX when in active growth. Good coverage is essential.

Grasses
When in active growth, spray with ZERO. For grass growing in amongst garden plants use GRASSKILLER.

9   Honeysuckle vine
When in full leaf and actively growing, spray with WOODY WEEDKILLER.

1   Ivy
When in full leaf, spray with WOODY WEEDKILLER; alternatively, paint liberally on freshly cut stump.

2   Kikuyu
When in full leaf and actively growing, spray with ZERO.

Moss in lawns and paths
Water or spray with SURRENDER. Use a pressure sprayer to achieve good penetration of the moss.

3   Onehunga weed
Spray with PRICKLE WEEDKILLER in spring from October onwards before the plant sets seed.

4   Onion weed
When in full leaf and actively growing, spray with AMITROLE and SPRAYFIX.

5   Oxalis
Sterilise soil with BASAMID in gardens where all plants can be removed while treating. Alternatively, when in full leaf spray with AMITROLE or ZERO. Repeat applications will be necessary.

6   Paspalum
When in full leaf, spray with ZERO.

7   Periwinkle
When in full leaf, spray with AMITROLE or WOODY WEEDKILLER.

8   Privet
Cut down and apply WOODY WEEDKILLER to freshly cut stump.

9   Wandering Jew
When in full leaf and growing vigorously, spray with AMITROLE and SPRAYFIX.

Willow
Cut a frill around the trunk and paint WOODY WEEDKILLER onto the exposed surface. Paint on stumps to prevent resprouting.

INSECTS

1 Praying mantis

The praying mantis feeds entirely on other insects, and as such is a boon to any garden. It frequently lurks in the foliage of shrubbery and scrub, and either waits for passing prey or hunts it down like a cat.

2 Lacewing

Lacewings and their larvae prey on small, soft-bodied insects, trapping them and sucking the juices from their bodies.

3 Ladybird

Almost all ladybirds are beneficial to the health of your garden. Both the adult and the larval forms feed on insects such as aphids, mites, scale and mealybugs. Although there are nearly thirty native species, some have been imported specifically as control agents, e.g. the steel-blue ladybird, the apple spider-mite ladybird and the bluegum scale ladybird. The decline of the ladybird population, perhaps as a result of indiscriminate spraying, is thought to have contributed to an increase in aphid infestations.

4 Ground beetle

The ground beetle preys on many harmful insects, and two species have been deliberately introduced to New Zealand as forms of biological control. It is frequently found in litter and debris on the ground, and is most active at night.

5 Tiger beetle

Like the ground beetle, the tiger beetle has a wide range of insect prey. It, too, forages in litter and ground debris, but is mostly active during the day. It can run at astonishing speed, and is even capable of catching flying insects.

6 Aphids

These small soft-bodied insects cluster on young shoots, flower buds or underneath leaves. Control with SHIELD, MAVRIK, SUPER SHIELD, NATURE'S WAY INSECT SPRAY or CONFIDOR.

1   Caterpillars

There are many types of caterpillars, which are usually the larval stage of moths or butterflies. Control with ORTHENE, MAVRIK, MALDISON, TARGET or PYRETHRUM.

2   Mealybug

These infest citrus trees, ornamentals and daphne, bulbs in storage and the roots of some plants. Control with CONFIDOR, SHIELD or ORTHENE.

3   Mites

The two-spotted mite attacks a wide range of fruit trees, vegetables and ornamentals. Control with MITE KILLER, MAVRIK, SUPER SHIELD or NATURE'S WAY INSECT SPRAY.

4   Passion vine hopper

These are damaging both in their adult form and their juvenile form, which is characterised by a white fluffy tail. Control with MALDISON or ORTHENE.

5   Scale

Scale insects are characterised by the waxy coating that protects the feeding insect. Control with CONQUEROR OIL, MALDISON, ORTHENE or CONFIDOR.

6   Green vegetable bug

The adult green vegetable bug plagues beans, tomatoes, potatoes, sweet corn, vine crops and sunflowers. Control with MAVRIK.

7   Thrips

At 1 mm long, thrips are just visible to the naked eye. They disfigure plants and transmit spotted wilt virus. Control with SUPER SHIELD, MAVRIK or CONFIDOR.

8   Weevil

Weevils damage plants by chewing stems and leaves. Control with MALDISON.

9   White fly

These small, sap-sucking insects attack annuals and vegetables, especially tomato, bean and vine crops. Control with TARGET, CONFIDOR, MAVRIK or NATURE'S WAY INSECT SPRAY.

FLOWERS

AFRICAN VIOLET

1 Yellow leaves

☹ Dry air. Too much sun. Incorrect watering. Overfeeding.

☺ Mist-spray plants. Move to new location. Monitor water and feeding carefully.

2 Pale green leaves with long stems

☹ Too cold.

☺ The minimum temperature should not be less than 15°C. Move pots away from windows on frosty nights.

Crown centre rotten. Limp leaves

☹ Crown rot.

☺ Remove and destroy infected plants. Do not overwater. Avoid temperature fluctuations.

No flowers

☹ Insufficient sunlight. Dry cold air.

☺ Move to new location with more light. If there is excessive leaf growth, remove some leaves to allow light into the crown.

3 Mouldy leaves and flowers

☹ Botrytis or powdery mildew.

☺ Pick off and destroy diseased parts. Spray with BAYCOR AEROSOL.

4 Straw-coloured patches on leaves

☹ Too much direct sun.

☺ Move to new location.

5 Brown spots on leaves

☹ Water damage.

☺ Keep water away from foliage, and water early in the day.

1 Tiny white insects on undersides of leaves which fly when disturbed

☹ Whitefly.

☺ Spray with NATURE'S WAY HOUSE PLANT SPRAY or CONFIDOR AEROSOL at three-day intervals.

2 Clusters of white cottony insects

☹ Mealybug.

☺ Wipe off with damp cloth. Spray with NATURE'S WAY HOUSE PLANT SPRAY or CONFIDOR AEROSOL. If badly infected, destroy plant.

3 Stunted leaves and twisted stems

☹ Mites.

☺ Spray with NATURE'S WAY HOUSE PLANT SPRAY, MAVRIK or MITE KILLER. If badly infected, destroy plant.

ANEMONE and RANUNCULUS

4 Insects clustered on young leaves

☹ Aphids.

☺ Keep plants well watered in dry conditions. Spray with CONFIDOR, NATURE'S WAY INSECT SPRAY or MAVRIK at first sign of infection.

5 Leaves yellow and orange-red pustules develop on undersides

☹ Rust.

☺ Spray with SHIELD, SUPER SHIELD, FUNGUS FIGHTER or GREENGUARD.

Bulbs fail to germinate or rot after shooting

☹ Pythium, damping-off.

☺ Disease is most prevalent in cold, wet soils. Dust bulbs with CAPTAN at planting time. Prepare soil well before planting, adding organic matter as necessary.

ASTER

1 Plant wilts, yellows and dies. Disease spreads from plant to plant

☹ Fusarium root rot.

☺ Burn plants with symptoms to avoid spread. Grow in a different area of garden each year or sterilise soil with BASAMID granules.

2 Leaves chewed

☹ Caterpillars.

☺ Spray with MAVRIK, SUPER SHIELD or NATURE'S WAY PYRETHRUM.

BEGONIA

3 Leaves and stems develop soft rots with grey or brown mould

☹ Botrytis, grey mould.

☺ A destructive disease in wet seasons. Remove mouldy leaves and badly infected plants. Improve ventilation. Spray with BRAVO or GREENGUARD.

4 Leaves develop spots of white powdery mould spreading over the whole surface

☹ Powdery mildew.

☺ Disease is encouraged by overcrowding and lack of soil moisture. Spray with SHIELD, SUPER SHIELD, FUNGUS FIGHTER or GREENGUARD at the first sign of infection.

5 Leaves become yellow and mottled and plants stunted. Fine webbing present on underside of leaf

☹ Mites.

☺ Common in hot dry conditions. Spray with MAVRIK, NATURE'S WAY INSECT SPRAY or MITE KILLER.

CALENDULA

6 Leaves develop a white powdery mildew

☹ Powdery mildew.

☺ Spray with SHIELD, SUPER SHIELD, FUNGUS FIGHTER or GREENGUARD.

CALLA LILY

1   Foliage collapses

☹ Bacterial soft rot of tubers (*Erwinia*).

☺ Avoid planting in wet, heavy soils. Destroy plants with infected tubers.

CARNATION (DIANTHUS)

2   Insects clustered on young leaves or flower buds

☹ Aphids.

☺ Keep plants well watered in dry weather. Spray with ORTHENE, CONFIDOR, MAVRIK, SHIELD, SUPER SHIELD or NATURE'S WAY INSECT SPRAY.

3   Leaves and flower buds with holes eaten

☹ Caterpillars.

☺ Spray with ORTHENE, MAVRIK, SHIELD or SUPER SHIELD.

4   Bud splitting

☹ Sudden and/or great temperature fluctuation. Excess fertiliser and/or water.

☺ Reduce fertiliser and water application to slow growth.

5   Twisted leaves and failure of flower buds to open

☹ Frost or snap of cold weather.

☺ Plant to avoid frosts.

6   Flecking in leaves and/or flowers

☹ Virus.

☺ Destroy plants.

7   Leaves yellow, wilt and die

☹ Fusarium wilt.

☺ Burn plants with symptoms. Plant carnations in different area of garden each year or sterilise soil with BASAMID.

1   **Red-brown pustules on leaves. Plant becomes stunted**

☹ Rust.

☺ Most prevalent in warm, humid weather. Spray with FUNGUS FIGHTER or GREENGUARD.

2   **Plants wilt and die rapidly**

☹ Sclerotinia stem rot.

☺ Remove and destroy infected plants. Avoid fluctuations in soil moisture and soils high in organic matter. Spray with GREENGUARD.

CHRYSANTHEMUM

3   **Leaves become silvery or yellow and dehydrated. Minute insects present**

☹ Mites.

☺ Most prevalent in warm weather. Spray with MAVRIK, NATURE'S WAY INSECT SPRAY or MITE KILLER.

4   **White pustules on undersides of leaves**

☹ White rust.

☺ Remove diseased leaves. Most common in moist weather. Spray with BRAVO, SHIELD, SUPER SHIELD or FUNGUS FIGHTER.

Plants wilt and die

☹ Fusarium or sclerotinia root rots.

☺ Sterilise soil with BASAMID.

5   **Wilting of plant. Leaves puckered and distorted. Insects under leaves or on new growth**

☹ Aphids.

☺ Spray with ORTHENE, CONFIDOR, MAVRIK, SHIELD, SUPER SHIELD or NATURE'S WAY INSECT SPRAY.

6   **Leaves develop black or brown patches, starting with lower leaves. Defoliation can occur**

☹ Nematodes (eelworm).

☺ Sterilise soil with BASAMID.

1 White, powdery mould on leaves

☹ Powdery mildew.

☺ Most prevalent in hot weather. Spray with SHIELD, SUPER SHIELD, GREENGUARD or FUNGUS FIGHTER at first sign of infection.

2 Leaves develop yellow spots. Orange or red pustules on undersides of leaves

☹ Brown rust.

☺ Remove and destroy diseased parts of plants. Spray with SHIELD, SUPER SHIELD, GREENGUARD or FUNGUS FIGHTER.

3 Pale or dark brown-black spots on leaves. Leaves may fall prematurely

☹ Leaf spot.

☺ Disease is worse in wet weather. Spray with SHIELD, SUPER SHIELD, GREENGUARD or FUNGUS FIGHTER.

CINERARIA

4 Leaves chewed and eaten

☹ Caterpillars.

☺ Spray with ORTHENE, MAVRIK, SHIELD or SUPER SHIELD.

5 Thin meandering lines through leaves

☹ Leafminer.

☺ Control weeds. Spray cinerarias regularly with ORTHENE or SHIELD.

6 White powdery mould on leaves

☹ Powdery mildew.

☺ Spray with SHIELD, SUPER SHIELD, GREENGUARD or FUNGUS FIGHTER. Disease establishes in conditions of high humidity.

CYCLAMEN

1 Leaves and stems develop soft, furry rot with grey-brown mould

☹ Botrytis, grey mould.

☺ Improve ventilation. Do not overwater or water leaves and stems. Remove infected leaves promptly. Spray with BRAVO or GREENGUARD.

2 Foliage droops

☹ Lack of moisture.

☺ Keep plants out of strong sun or heat. Mist-spray foliage in dry conditions.

3 Yellow foliage

☹ Too hot and/or dry.

☺ Avoid extreme temperatures and underwatering.

4 Plant collapses

☹ Overwatering, causing crown rot.

☺ Never let water stand on fleshy crown.

5 Twisted, stunted leaves. Flower buds wither

☹ Mites.

☺ More prevalent in warm weather. Spray with NATURE'S WAY INSECT SPRAY, MAVRIK or MITE KILLER.

Short flowering period

☹ Too warm, too dry. Lack of fertiliser.

☺ Feed with THRIVE FLOWER & FRUIT or LUSH HOUSE PLANT FOOD and water regularly during growing and flowering period.

DAFFODIL and JONQUIL (NARCISSI)

6 Larvae burrowing in bulbs, which fail to grow. Infected bulbs feel light and soft

☹ Bulb fly.

☺ Destroy infested bulbs. Spray foliage with ORTHENE during spring and summer. After foliage has died down, cultivate soil to ensure top of bulb is covered and not exposed. Work SOIL INSECT KILLER granules into soil.

1 Mottling, yellow-brown streaks

🙁 Virus.

🙂 Destroy infected plants.

2 Twisted leaves with ridges

🙁 Nematodes.

🙂 Destroy infected bulbs. Sterilise soil with BASAMID.

DAHLIA

3 Holes in leaves and flower buds

🙁 Caterpillars.

🙂 Spray with ORTHENE, MAVRIK, SHIELD or SUPER SHIELD.

4 Leaves develop spots of white powdery mould, which spreads over the whole surface

🙁 Powdery mildew.

🙂 Most prevalent in hot, dry weather. Spray with SHIELD, SUPER SHIELD, GREENGUARD or FUNGUS FIGHTER.

Stems or whole plants wilt and collapse

🙁 Verticillium root and stem rot.

🙂 Remove and burn infected plants. Sterilise soil with BASAMID granules between plantings, or plant in different area. Improve drainage to reduce chance of infection.

5 Flowers and foliage nibbled

🙁 Earwigs.

🙂 Clean up leaf litter and other debris on ground. Spray with ORTHENE or PYRETHRUM.

Soft, weak leaves, reduced flowering

🙁 Excess nitrogen fertiliser.

🙂 Use a balanced fertiliser, e.g. GRO-PLUS COMPLETE PLANT FOOD.

1 **Yellow-green spots on leaves**

☹ Leaf spot.

☺ Worse in cool humid weather. Spray with FUNGUS FIGHTER or GREENGUARD.

2 **Leaves yellow (stippled or mottled), becoming dehydrated. Fine webbing present on underside of leaves**

☹ Mites.

☺ Spray with MAVRIK, NATURE'S WAY INSECT SPRAY, SUPER SHIELD or MITE KILLER.

DELPHINIUM

3 **Wilting of plant. Leaves puckered and distorted. Insects under leaves or on new growth**

☹ Aphids.

☺ Keep plants well watered in dry weather. Spray with MAVRIK, SUPER SHIELD, CONFIDOR or NATURE'S WAY INSECT SPRAY.

4 **Leaves develop spots of white mould**

☹ Powdery mildew.

☺ Most common in hot, dry weather. Spray with SHIELD, SUPER SHIELD, GREENGUARD or FUNGUS FIGHTER.

GERANIUM (PELARGONIUM)

5 **Small, pale green spots on upper leaf surface, with brown spores on lower leaf**

☹ Rust.

☺ Remove infected leaves. Spray with SHIELD, SUPER SHIELD, GREENGUARD or FUNGUS FIGHTER. Do not apply excessive quantities of nitrogen.

6 **Brown sunken spots. Leaves yellow, fall**

☹ Leaf spot.

☺ Favoured by warm, wet weather. Remove infected leaves promptly. Avoid overhead watering. Spray with FUNGUS FIGHTER or GREENGUARD.

1 Flowers become spotted and then rot

☹ Botrytis, grey mould.

☺ Most common when weather is wet or humid. Remove infected parts. Spray with BRAVO or GREENGUARD.

2 Chewed leaves

☹ Caterpillars.

☺ Spray with MAVRIK, ORTHENE, SHIELD or SUPER SHIELD.

3 Wilting of plant. Leaves puckered and distorted. Insects under leaves or on new growth

☹ Aphids.

☺ Spray with MAVRIK, SHIELD, SUPER SHIELD, CONFIDOR or PYRETHRUM.

4 Upper leaf surface speckled with yellow blotches. Leaves fall prematurely

☹ Mites.

☺ Spray with MAVRIK, SUPER SHIELD, NATURE'S WAY INSECT SPRAY or MITE KILLER.

5 Undersides of leaves covered with tiny white insects, which fly when disturbed

☹ Whitefly.

☺ Spray with CONFIDOR, SUPER SHIELD, TARGET, MAVRIK or NATURE'S WAY INSECT SPRAY at first sign of infection, and then at regular intervals.

6 Stunting of plant, yellowing leaves

☹ Nematodes.

☺ Destroy plant. Sterilise soil with BASAMID.

7 Yellow, curling leaves

☹ Virus.

☺ Destroy plant. Control aphids to prevent infection.

GERBERA

1 Brown spots with purplish ring

☹ Leaf spot.

☺ Most common in late summer. Spread by wind and rain. Remove diseased material. Spray with FUNGUS FIGHTER or GREENGUARD.

2 Brown, spreading rot

☹ Sclerotinia.

☺ Improve drainage. Destroy infected plants. Sterilise soil with BASAMID. Spray with GREENGUARD.

3 Leaves yellow and die. Plant dies back

☹ Phytophthora.

☺ Improve drainage. Destroy infected plants. Sterilise soil with BASAMID.

4 White pustules appear on lower leaf surfaces

☹ White rust.

☺ Remove and burn infected leaves. Spray with SHIELD, SUPER SHIELD, GREENGUARD or FUNGUS FIGHTER.

GLADIOLUS

5 Dry appearance, silvering on upper sides of leaves, brown streaks on undersides. Flowers distorted and only partially opened, colour-streaked and speckled

☹ Thrips.

☺ Hot, dry conditions favour this insect. Overhead watering reduces number. Spray with MAVRIK, SHIELD, SUPER SHIELD, CONFIDOR or ORTHENE. Add SPRAYFIX for improved control.

6 Flowers, leaves and stems develop water-soaked spots and grey-brown mould

☹ Botrytis, grey mould.

☺ Destroy diseased plants. Spray with BRAVO or GREENGUARD.

1 **Brown, pitted patches on corms**

☹ Fusarium rot.

☺ Store in dry, airy place. Dust with sulphur. Sterilise soil with BASAMID or avoid planting in wet or diseased soil.

HOLLYHOCK

2 **Tiny white insects under leaves which fly when disturbed**

☹ Whitefly.

☺ Spray regularly with MAVRIK, SUPER SHIELD, CONFIDOR, NATURE'S WAY INSECT SPRAY or TARGET.

3 **Leaves yellow (stippled or mottled), becoming dehydrated. Fine webbing on undersides of leaves**

☹ Mites.

☺ Most common in warm weather. Spray with MAVRIK, SUPER SHIELD, MITE KILLER or NATURE'S WAY INSECT SPRAY.

HOUSEPLANTS

4 **Wilting of plant. Leaves puckered and distorted. Insects under leaves or on new growth**

☹ Aphids.

☺ Keep plants evenly watered over summer. Spray with NATURE'S WAY HOUSEPLANT SPRAY (MISTETTE or AEROSOL) or CONFIDOR AEROSOL.

5 **White, cottony or waxy insects on the undersides of leaves and leaf axils. Plants do not thrive**

☹ Mealybug.

☺ Control is difficult. If only a few are present wipe off with a damp cloth. Otherwise spray with NATURE'S WAY HOUSEPLANT SPRAY AEROSOL or CONFIDOR AEROSOL. Discard heavily infested plants.

1 **Stems and flowers covered with flattened red, grey or brown scaly bumps**

☹ Scale.

☺ Spray with CONFIDOR AEROSOL. Repeat applications may be necessary. Spray outdoors.

2 **Leaves yellow, become stippled and may fall. Fine webbing may be present**

☹ Mites.

☺ Most common in warm, dry conditions. Spray with MAVRIK, SUPER SHIELD, MITE KILLER or NATURE'S WAY INSECT SPRAY at regular intervals.

3 **Brown spots on leaves, flowers and sometimes stems. Fuzzy grey growth and rot may be present**

☹ Botrytis.

☺ Diseased and dead plant material should be removed promptly, particularly flowers. Avoid splashing water on foliage and growing plants in crowded conditions where the air is damp and still. Spray with BRAVO or GREENGUARD.

4 **Leaves small and pale. Flowers poor or absent. Lower leaves turn yellow, dry and fall. Spindly growth with long spaces between leaves. Variegated leaves turn green**

☹ Too little light.

☺ Place in a better-lit situation.

5 **Leaves limp. Soft areas may appear. Poor growth. Leaves curl, yellow and wilt. Tips may brown**

☹ Too much water.

☺ Reduce watering. (This is particularly important in winter.)

6 **Leaves curl, brown and fall**

☹ Too cold.

☺ Place in warmer situation.

Spindly growth when in good light conditions. Flowers are short lived. Lower leaves wilt, brown and fall

☹ Too hot.

☺ Place in another position.

1 Pale leaves, weak growth

☹ Lack of fertiliser.

☺ Feed with NUTRICOTE INDOOR & PATIO fertiliser. Apply LUSH HOUSE PLANT FOOD, NITROSOL or BIO-GOLD regularly.

2 Leaves fall after rapid yellowing

☹ Rapid change in temperature.

☺ Regulate temperature.

3 Leaf tips brown and shrivel. Leaf edges yellow. Buds and flowers shrivel and fall

☹ Dry air.

☺ Mist-spray with water to increase humidity or sit plant on saucer filled with gravel chips and water.

4 Leaves turn yellow and fall. Brown tips or edges on leaves

☹ Draughts.

☺ Position away from draughts.

IRIS

5 Red spots on leaves

☹ Rust.

☺ Common in warm, humid conditions. Spray with SHIELD, SUPER SHIELD, GREENGUARD or FUNGUS FIGHTER.

6 Brown spots which run together to form large dead areas

☹ Leaf spot.

☺ Worst in warm, wet weather. Remove infected parts. Spray with FUNGUS FIGHTER, BRAVO or GREENGUARD.

1 Yellow streaks on foliage
☹ Virus.
☺ Destroy infected plants.

2 Rotting leaf bases
☹ Bacterial rot.
☺ Destroy infected plants. Improve drainage and sterilise soil with BASAMID granules.

LILY

3 Insects clustered on young leaves, causing distortion
☹ Aphids.
☺ Spray with CONFIDOR, ORTHENE, MAVRIK, SHIELD or SUPER SHIELD.

4 Plants wilt and die back. Bulbs rot
☹ Fusarium, rhizoctonia or phytophthora root rots.
☺ Most common in heavy wet soils. Plant only in free-draining soils. Treat bulbs with CAPTAN before planting.

MARIGOLD

5 Browning and decay of the flower
☹ Botrytis, blight.
☺ Pick off and destroy browned flowers. Spray with BRAVO or GREENGUARD.

6 Lower leaves develop oval, blackish spots
☹ Leaf spot.
☺ Spray with GREENGUARD or FUNGUS FIGHTER.

7 Rotting at the crown or roots of plant. Browning of stems and wilting of plants
☹ Root rot. Fusarium or phytophthora wilt.
☺ Most common in heavy, wet soils. Plant only in free-draining situations.

1 Yellow or orange pustules on leaves

☹ Rust.

☺ Common in warm, humid weather. Remove infected plants quickly. Spray with SHIELD, SUPER SHIELD, GREENGUARD or FUNGUS FIGHTER.

2 Leaves yellow (stippled or mottled), becoming dehydrated. Fine webbing present on undersides of leaves

☹ Mites.

☺ Spray with MAVRIK, SUPER SHIELD, NATURE'S WAY INSECT SPRAY or MITE KILLER.

NEMESIA

3 Plants wilt and die. Stems rot at ground level

☹ Fusarium or sclerotinia root rot.

☺ More common in heavy wet soils. Plant only in free-draining situations.

ORCHID

4 Small insects clustered on new growth

☹ Aphids.

☺ Keep plants evenly watered. Spray with CONFIDOR, SHIELD, SUPER SHIELD or MAVRIK.

5 Young leaves or flower buds eaten

☹ Slugs and snails.

☺ Lay BLITZEM (pellets or granules) or MESUROL.

6 Yellow or brownish mottling of leaves

☹ Mites, thrips.

☺ Spray with MAVRIK or SUPER SHIELD.

7 Whitish, cotton wool-like tufts on leaves and pseudo bulbs

☹ Mealybug.

☺ Spray with ORTHENE, SHIELD or CONFIDOR.

1 Black spots

☹ Glomerella.

☺ Avoid overhead watering, reduce humidity and improve ventilation. Spray with GREENGUARD.

2 Flowers deformed and semi-transparent patches on leaves

☹ Virus.

☺ Destroy affected plants.

3 Small, brown, flattened scales on leaves and pseudo bulbs. Leaves yellow and stop growing

☹ Scale.

☺ Pick off scale to remove small infestations. Spray with CONQUEROR OIL and CONFIDOR.

4 Yellow-brown leaves, sometimes with brown, drying patches

☹ Scorching due to lack of shading and proper ventilation during hot weather.

☺ Shade in spring and ensure adequate ventilation.

5 Rot in growing point. Leaf base blackens

☹ Bacterial rot.

☺ Avoid overhead watering, reduce humidity and improve ventilation. Destroy infected bulbs.

6 Flower buds fail to develop properly, usually withering or falling early

☹ Too cold or too hot and dry.

☺ Moderate extremes in temperature.

7 Brown speckling on young leaves, petals

☹ Excessive humidity.

☺ Improve ventilation on warm days.

8 Small yellow leaves; few or no flowers

☹ Nutrient deficiency.

☺ Re-pot using specialised orchid potting mix. When watering, liquid feed with LUSH ORCHID FOOD or THRIVE ALL PURPOSE.

PANSY and VIOLA

1 Insects clustered on young leaves

☹ Aphids.

☺ Water regularly in dry weather. Spray with CONFIDOR, MAVRIK, NATURE'S WAY INSECT SPRAY, SHIELD or SUPER SHIELD.

2 Leaves develop stippled or mottled yellowing and become dehydrated in hot, dry weather

☹ Mites.

☺ Spray with MAVRIK, MITE KILLER, SUPER SHIELD or NATURE'S WAY INSECT SPRAY.

3 White, powdery mould on leaves, particularly in summer or autumn

☹ Powdery mildew.

☺ More prevalent in hot, dry weather. Spray with SHIELD, SUPER SHIELD, GREENGUARD or FUNGUS FIGHTER.

4 Leaves yellow and develop red pustules underneath

☹ Rust.

☺ Spray with SHIELD, SUPER SHIELD, GREENGUARD or FUNGUS FIGHTER.

PETUNIA

A black discolouration and dry rot of crown. Wilting

☹ Crown rot.

☺ Destroy plants. Sterilise soil with BASAMID.

5 Plants wilt and die

☹ Sclerotinia or other root rots.

☺ Sterilise soil with BASAMID or grow in a different area. Spray with GREENGUARD.

6 Spreading white mould on leaves

☹ Powdery mildew.

☺ Spray with SHIELD, SUPER SHIELD, GREENGUARD or FUNGUS FIGHTER.

ROSE

1 **Tiny green or pink soft-bodied insects on leaves, stems and buds. Flower buds may look deformed and not open properly**

☹ Aphids.

☺ Spray with SHIELD, SUPER SHIELD, MAVRIK or CONFIDOR

2 **Yellowing speckling of leaves, white webbing underneath, severe leaf drop**

☹ Mites.

☺ More common in hot, dry conditions. Spray with SUPER SHIELD, MAVRIK or MITE KILLER at first sign. Spray with CONQUEROR OIL in winter as a preventative measure.

3 **Hard, grey-white, scale-like insects on woody and green stems. Poor growth, pale, dehydrated leaves**

☹ Scale.

☺ Prune badly infected stems and burn. Spray with CONFIDOR in summer and CONQUEROR OIL in winter.

4 **Leaves silvery, with distortion and browning of petals. Flower buds deformed and may not open. Flowers have shrivelled petals**

☹ Thrips.

☺ Remove infested buds and blooms. As a preventative measure, spray with SHIELD, SUPER SHIELD, MAVRIK or CONFIDOR when weather is warm and dry.

5 **Circular black spots on upper leaf surface. Leaves may drop prematurely. Flowering may decrease. Stems may become infected**

☹ Black spot.

☺ Remove spent flowers, fallen leaves and prunings. From early spring spray every two weeks with SHIELD or SUPER SHIELD, alternating with BRAVO or GREENGUARD. Particularly prevalent in warm, humid weather. Prune to increase air movement through plants.

1   Maroon or black blotches, usually confined to the veins. In humid weather a furry growth may appear on undersides

☹   Downy mildew (symptoms similar to black spot, but usually occurring earlier).

☺   Cool, moist conditions encourage rapid spread. Keep foliage as dry as possible. Spray with BRAVO or GREENGUARD in spring and autumn.

2   Yellow patches on upper leaf surface, with orange pustules underneath

☹   Rust.

☺   Spray with SHIELD or SUPER SHIELD, alternating with GREENGUARD or BRAVO.

3   New growth appears distorted with whitish grey powder

☹   Powdery mildew.

☺   Keep plants well watered as disease is favoured by dry root conditions. Spray with SHIELD or SUPER SHIELD, alternating with GREENGUARD or BRAVO.

4   Silvering of leaves; plants do not thrive

☹   Silverleaf.

☺   Remove and burn all infected wood on a dry day. Thoroughly sterilise secateurs after pruning infected plants. Seal pruning cuts with BACSEAL PRUNING PAINT.

5   Small, irregular, colourless spots on foliage. Stunted growth. Yellowing most common on older plants

☹   Virus.

☺   Destroy infected plants to prevent spread. Purchase High Health plants.

1 **Leaves yellow and/or develop dark purple tones. Leaves are small and drop prematurely. Slow, weak or stunted growth**

☹ Lack of fertiliser.

☺ Fertilise regularly with GRO-PLUS ROSE FOOD, NUTRICOTE OUTDOOR & SHRUB, BIO-GOLD, BIO-GOLD ORGANIC PELLETS, LUSH or THRIVE ALL PURPOSE.

SNAPDRAGON

Plants wilt and die. Occurs more in poorly drained, wet soils

☹ Phytophthora, sclerotinia or verticillium root rot.

☺ Improve drainage by incorporating generous quantities of peat. Destroy infected plants.

2 **Yellowing of leaves, red pustules under leaves**

☹ Rust.

☺ Most common in cool, humid weather. Spray with SHIELD, SUPER SHIELD, GREENGUARD or FUNGUS FIGHTER.

3 **Yellowing of leaves with pale pitting or patches. Grey-brown on undersides**

☹ Downy mildew.

☺ Spray with FUNGUS FIGHTER or GREENGUARD.

4 **Brown leaf spots**

☹ Leaf spot.

☺ Spray with BRAVO or GREENGUARD.

STOCK

5 **Wilting of plant. Leaves puckered and distorted. Insects under leaves or on new growth**

☹ Aphids.

☺ Spray with SHIELD, SUPER SHIELD, MAVRIK, CONFIDOR or NATURE'S WAY INSECT SPRAY.

1 Leaves develop pale, pitted patches or spots with grey mould on undersides. Occurs mainly in spring and autumn

☹ Downy mildew.

☺ Most serious in cool, humid weather. Spray with BRAVO or GREENGUARD.

2 Whitish powder on leaf surface

☹ Powdery mildew.

☺ Spray with SHIELD, SUPER SHIELD, GREENGUARD or FUNGUS FIGHTER.

3 Plants fail to grow; wilt and die

☹ Fusarium, phytophthora or verticillium root rot.

☺ Destroy infected plants. Sterilise soil with BASAMID or plant only in well-drained soils.

SWEET PEA

4 White, dusty coating on foliage

☹ Powdery mildew.

☺ Prevalent in hot, dry weather. Spray with SHIELD, SUPER SHIELD, GREENGUARD or FUNGUS FIGHTER.

Poor germination

☹ Pythium.

☺ Avoid planting in cold, damp soils. Add BLACK MAGIC SEED-RAISING MIX to soil when sowing seeds in the garden.

TREES, SHRUBS AND LAWNS

AZALEA, CAMELLIA and RHODODENDRON

1 Clusters of insects on young growth

☹ Aphids.

☺ Keep plants watered in dry weather. Spray with MAVRIK, NATURE'S WAY INSECT SPRAY or CONFIDOR.

2 Yellow speckling of leaves, white webbing on undersides, dry appearance

☹ Mites.

☺ Keep well watered; hose leaf undersides. Treat with MAVRIK, NATURE'S WAY INSECT SPRAY or MITE KILLER.

3 Leaves silver, become brittle and dry. Brown-black specks appear on underside of leaves

☹ Thrips.

☺ Control weeds. Overhead watering will reduce numbers. Spray with MAVRIK, CONFIDOR or ORTHENE at first sign of infestation.

4 Black, sooty mould on leaves and twigs

☹ Sooty mould.

☺ Sooty mould fungus lives on honeydew secreted from sap-sucking insects. Spray with MAVRIK or ORTHENE to control insects.

5 New leaves and flowers are thickened, fleshy, pale green. Thickenings enlarge and become white or pink, with a powdery appearance during wet weather

☹ Leaf gall.

☺ Remove and burn all infected parts.

6 Leaves yellow and/or develop dark purple tone. Slow, stunted growth

☹ Lack of fertiliser.

☺ Fertilise with GRO-PLUS CAMELLIA & AZALEA FOOD in late spring after flowering finishes and just before buds form in autumn.

1 Decline in vigour and leaves turn yellow while the veins remain green

🙁 Soil too alkaline, making iron unavailable.

🙂 Fertilise with GRO-PLUS CAMELLIA & AZALEA FOOD or GRO-PLUS IRON SULPHATE in spring before new growth starts. Do not lime. Plants in concrete tubs or planted by new paths may have problems.

2 Long, silvery, grey, dead areas on leaves

🙁 Pestalotiopsis.

🙂 Fungus invades areas on leaves that are sunburnt or physically damaged. Avoid damaging leaves in this way.

3 New shoots die back

🙁 Dieback.

🙂 Fungus invades plant through a wound, killing the tissue and forming a canker. Prune off infected parts and seal with BACSEAL PRUNING PAINT.

BOTTLEBRUSH (CALLISTEMON)

4 Young leaves webbed together with holes and a tatty appearance

🙁 Leaf roller caterpillar.

🙂 Spray with ORTHENE or MAVRIK.

5 Leaves become distorted, tightly rolled, red-brown and brittle

🙁 Thrips.

🙂 Damage most obvious in autumn. Spray with CONFIDOR, MAVRIK, SHIELD or ORTHENE.

Small brown discs on stem

🙁 Scale.

🙂 Spray with CONFIDOR or ORTHENE.

CONIFER

1 Leaves webbed together. Presence of a soft woven case, containing a grub-like insect

🙁 Case moth.

🙂 Spray with ORTHENE or MAVRIK.

Branches of cypress trees die back. Resin oozes from branches

🙁 Cypress canker.

🙂 *Chamaecyparis* and *Cupressus* are susceptible. Remove affected trees; replant other species.

2 Die-back starting on the inner foliage and moving out. Odd branches dying

🙁 Phytophthora or sclerotinia root rot.

🙂 Improve drainage. Plant resistant species. Spray with GREENGUARD.

ELM

3 Yellowing, wilting and browning of leaves on branches that eventually die. Stripping the tree bark reveals brown streaks in the sap wood

🙁 Dutch elm disease.

🙂 If you suspect you have an infected tree contact the Ministry of Agriculture and Forestry, who will arrange for the tree to be inspected. If found to be infected, the tree will have to be removed and destroyed.

FERN

4 Poor growth. Brown scales on fronds

🙁 Scale.

🙂 Spray with CONFIDOR or ORTHENE. Use with caution on tender foliage.

5 Yellowing, limp fronds

🙁 Air too warm and/or incorrect watering.

🙂 Place in cooler position and monitor watering more carefully.

1 Brown tips on fronds

☹ Dry air.

☺ Mist-spray regularly or move to a new location.

2 White, cottony masses

☹ Mealybug.

☺ Keep plants well watered and well fed. Destroy plant if badly infected. Spray with CONFIDOR or ORTHENE. Use with caution on tender foliage.

FICUS (ORNAMENTAL FIG, e.g. RUBBER PLANT, TRAILING FIG, WEEPING FIG)

Sudden loss of leaves

☹ Overwatering. Too cold, too dark.

☺ Move to a new location. Water only when surface of potting mix is dry to the touch.

3 Loss of lower leaves

☹ Natural ageing process or overwatering.

☺ Reduce watering.

4 Yellowing leaf edges

☹ Underfeeding.

☺ Feed regularly with THRIVE ALL PURPOSE, LUSH ALL PURPOSE, BIO-GOLD or NUTRICOTE INDOOR & PATIO.

5 Dry, shrivelled leaves

☹ Exposure to direct sunlight. Air too dry.

☺ Keep out of direct sun. Mist-spray leaves.

6 Leaves mottled yellow or silvery with brown specks on undersides

☹ Mites or thrips.

☺ Most prevalent in hot, dry conditions. Spray with MAVRIK, NATURE'S WAY INSECT SPRAY, MITE KILLER or SUPER SHIELD.

1 Small brown discs on undersides of leaves. Poor growth

☹ Scale.

☺ Common in dry conditions. Spray or wipe with CONQUEROR OIL and CONFIDOR.

FLAX

2 Brown or red spots on leaves

☹ Leaf spot.

☺ Spray with FUNGUS FIGHTER or GREENGUARD.

3 Leaf tissue chewed from underside in long strips, exposing the fibre

☹ Flax caterpillar.

☺ Spray with ORTHENE, MAVRIK or TARGET.

4 Colonies of soft, white or pink scale, usually near the base or lower leaves

☹ Scale.

☺ Common in dry conditions. Spray with CONFIDOR and CONQUEROR OIL in spring and autumn. Spray must penetrate leaf bases.

FUCHSIA

5 Wilting of plant. Leaves puckered and distorted. Insects under leaves or on new growth

☹ Aphids.

☺ Keep plants well watered in dry weather. Spray with CONFIDOR, MAVRIK, ORTHENE or NATURE'S WAY INSECT SPRAY.

6 Leaves silvery and dehydrated. Undersides covered with brown specks

☹ Thrips.

☺ Spray with CONFIDOR, MAVRIK, ORTHENE or SUPER SHIELD.

7 Yellow leaves. Orange or red pustules develop on undersides

☹ Rust.

☺ Remove infected leaves. Spray with GREENGUARD or FUNGUS FIGHTER.

GUM (EUCALYPTUS)

1 Young leaves webbed together. Leaves chewed with a tatty appearance

☹ Leaf roller caterpillar.

☺ Spray with ORTHENE, MAVRIK, SHIELD or SUPER SHIELD.

2 Leaves eaten and severely damaged. Presence of large blue-green caterpillar

☹ Emperor gum moth.

☺ Spray with ORTHENE, MAVRIK, SHIELD or SUPER SHIELD.

3 Young trees develop stem and leaf rot with grey mould

☹ Botrytis, grey mould

☺ Common in wet, humid weather. Spray with BRAVO or GREENGUARD.

4 Brown or red spots on leaves

☹ Leaf spot

☺ Spray with FUNGUS FIGHTER or GREENGUARD.

HEBE

5 Pale, clearly defined leaf spots

☹ Septoria leaf spot.

☺ Prevalent in wet, humid weather. Spray with BRAVO or GREENGUARD.

6 Leaves develop yellow areas which spread and turn black

☹ Downy mildew.

☺ Prevalent during wet weather in spring. Spray with BRAVO or GREENGUARD.

7 Severe blackening, die back, wilting and death of plant

☹ Phytophthora or sclerotinia root rot.

☺ Destroy plant. Sterilise soil with BASAMID. Improve drainage. Plant resistant species. Spray with GREENGUARD.

IVY

1 Small brown 'scales' attached to plant. Plant does not thrive

☹ Scale.

☺ More common in dry conditions. Spray with CONQUEROR OIL and ORTHENE or CONFIDOR.

2 Brown spots on foliage. Leaves yellow and fall from plant

☹ Leaf spot.

☺ Most common in cool, damp situations. Remove and burn diseased leaves. Spray with FUNGUS FIGHTER or GREENGUARD.

3 Small insects feeding on new growth and causing distortion

☹ Aphids.

☺ More common in dry conditions. Spray with CONFIDOR, NATURE'S WAY INSECT SPRAY, MAVRIK or SUPER SHIELD.

KOWHAI

4 Leaves severely stripped. Presence of bright-green and black caterpillar

☹ Kowhai caterpillar.

☺ Only a problem if the population grows excessively. Spray with ORTHENE, MAVRIK, SHIELD or SUPER SHIELD.

LAWN

5 Grass ceases to thrive and may die in autumn or early spring. Turf comes out because of root damage

☹ Grass grub.

☺ Most common on sandy or volcanic soils. Apply SOIL INSECT KILLER granules in February when the grubs are young and near the surface. Water granules in thoroughly.

1 Grass ceases to thrive, browns and dies in summer. Both root and crown damage are apparent

☹ Black beetle.

☺ Most common in northern areas with volcanic or sandy soils. Apply SOIL INSECT KILLER granules.

2 Leaves and crown eaten. Presence of worm-like casts. Caterpillars can be found in vertical burrows in autumn

☹ Porina caterpillar.

☺ Use SOIL INSECT KILLER granules in autumn to control the young caterpillars before they begin to grow.

3 Presence of a large quantity of worm casts causing a muddy surface

☹ Earthworms.

☺ Remove clippings when mowing. Do not lime, but topdress with peat to keep soil acid.

4 Purplish, circular or irregular patches which turn brown and die

☹ Brown patch

☺ Reduce application of nitrogen fertiliser. Spray with GREENGUARD.

5 Small patches of 'cobwebs' on turf show up under dewy conditions, then turn brown

☹ Fusarium patch.

☺ Most common in humid conditions. Avoid nitrogenous fertiliser in winter. Spray with GREENGUARD.

6 Mottled patches of grass. Distinctive bright red threads of fungal growth

☹ Red thread.

☺ Fertilise lawn in spring and autumn. Avoid mowing too closely. Spray with FUNGUS FIGHTER or GREENGUARD.

1 Pale grass. Plants collapse in circles

☹ Pythium, damping-off.

☺ Common in new lawns. Do not overseed. Keep seed moist, but avoid overwatering. Do not use nitrogenous fertilisers on new lawns.

2 Rings of dead grass which get larger each year. May have a ring of puff balls associated with them

☹ Fairy rings.

☺ Spray with GREENGUARD or FUNGUS FIGHTER.

3 Pale green grass with weed dominance

☹ Lack of fertiliser.

☺ Fertilise in spring and autumn with fertiliser blended for lawns, e.g. GRO-PLUS PROFESSIONAL LAWN FOOD.

4 Weeds

☹ Poor condition.

☺ Fertilise in spring and autumn. Keep evenly watered over summer. Do not mow too closely. Spray with TURFIX LAWN WEED SPRAY or WEED 'N' FEED.

5 Slippery, green patches of moss

☹ Moss.

☺ Improve drainage, aeration and exposure to sunlight. Spray with SURRENDER. Fertilise in spring and autumn.

LEUCODENDRON

6 Plant wilts and dies. Black dieback may be present

☹ Phytophthora root rot.

☺ Plant only in free-draining situations.

7 Plant silvers and ceases to thrive

☹ Silver leaf.

☺ Prune out infected wood on a dry day and burn. Seal wounds with BACSEAL PRUNING PAINT.

MANUKA (LEPTOSPERMUM)

1 Sooty, black mould covering plant. Dead branches may look as if they have suffered fire damage

☹ Manuka blight caused by sucking insects, scale and mealybug, producing a honeydew secretion on which the sooty mould grows.

☺ Spray with CONFIDOR or ORTHENE and CONQUEROR OIL to control insects.

2 Leaves webbed together, often eaten or tatty

☹ Leaf roller caterpillar.

☺ Spray with ORTHENE, MAVRIK or SHIELD.

NANDINA

3 Yellow, poor growth

☹ Virus.

☺ Purchase plants labelled 'High-Health'. Control insects to help prevent infection.

OLEANDER

4 Rough, woody galls appear on leaves

☹ Bacterial oleander gall.

☺ Prune off all galls and destroy. Keep plant growing vigorously with regular fertilising and watering.

5 Rough, white scales on underside of leaves

☹ Oleander scale.

☺ Spray with CONQUEROR OIL and CONFIDOR or ORTHENE.

PALM

6 White, cottony areas on fronds

☹ Mealybug.

☺ Remove small infestations with a damp cloth. Spray with ORTHENE or CONFIDOR.

1 **Small, brown discs attached to leaves and stems or white scaly material on underside of leaves**

☹ Scale.

☺ Prune off infected fronds or destroy badly infected plants. Spray with ORTHENE or CONFIDOR.

2 **Leaves brown at tips**

☹ Dry air, underwatering and cold air.

☺ Mist-spray plant, monitor watering and keep plants away from cold draughts.

3 **Brown leaves**

☹ Overwatering.

☺ Monitor watering.

4 **Brown spots**

☹ Overwatering. Chilling. Hard water.

☺ Remove affected foliage and improve growing conditions.

PHEBALIUM

5 **Plants wilt and die**

☹ Phytophthora collar rot.

☺ Avoid clay soils. Plant resistant species.

PHOTINIA

6 **Leaves eaten**

☹ Caterpillars.

☺ Spray with CONFIDOR, SHIELD, SUPER SHIELD, MAVRIK or ORTHENE.

7 **Leaves become silvery and dehydrated with brown specks on undersides**

☹ Thrips.

☺ Spray with SHIELD, SUPER SHIELD, MAVRIK, ORTHENE or CONFIDOR.

PITTOSPORUM

1   Distortion, crinkling or pitting of young leaves. Presence of sooty black mould

☹ Psyllid.

☺ Spray with ORTHENE or SHIELD.

POHUTUKAWA

2   Distortion, crinkling or pitting of young leaves

☹ Psyllid.

☺ Spray with ORTHENE or SHIELD.

POPLAR

3   Leaves yellow in summer and drop prematurely

☹ Rust.

☺ Plant rust-resistant poplar varieties, e.g. 'Flevo' or '2001'

VEGETABLES AND HERBS

ASPARAGUS

1 Plant wilts, yellows and dies

☹ Fusarium or phytophthora root rot.

☺ Worse in heavy wet soils. Plant only healthy crowns in free-draining soils. Plant resistant varieties, e.g. 'MaryWashington'.

AVOCADO

2 Leaves wilt, yellow and die. Branches die back from tip

☹ Phytophthora root rot.

☺ Ensure good drainage. Avoid clay soils. Avoid overwatering.

Flowers fall

☹ Reduced fruit set.

☺ Avoid fertilising during flowering.

3 Small leaves, crowded with yellowing between veins

☹ Zinc deficiency.

☺ When actively growing, spray foliage with THRIVE ALL PURPOSE or LUSH ALL PURPOSE and apply GRO-PLUS TRACE ELEMENT MIX.

4 Leaves folded or webbed together. Chewed skin on fruit; forms brown scars

☹ Leaf roller caterpillar.

☺ Spray with CARBARYL or TARGET.

5 Circular spots on fruit, which enlarge and darken. Rot spreads through flesh

☹ Anthracnose.

☺ Spores spread in warm, wet weather. Handle fruit carefully to avoid damage. Store in a cool, well-ventilated area. Spray with CHAMPION COPPER at monthly intervals from flowering to harvest. Prune out dead twigs.

BEAN — DWARF & CLIMBING

1 Holes in bean pods

☹ Tomato fruit worm.

☺ Protect young plants by spraying with TARGET, MALDISON or CARBARYL.

2 Circular, yellow spots on leaves and stems

☹ Rust.

☺ Infection favoured by cool, damp weather. Remove badly infected plants and destroy. Use rust-tolerant varieties, e.g. 'Mangere Pole'. Spray with BRAVO.

3 Leaves eaten mainly on undersides. Leaves and pods rough

☹ Looper or other caterpillars. Vegetable or shield bug.

☺ Protect young plants by spraying with TARGET or CARBARYL.

Young growing tips deformed with clusters of insects

☹ Aphids.

☺ Keep plants well watered in dry weather. Spray with TARGET or NATURE'S WAY INSECT SPRAY.

Failure of plants to emerge or weak distorted seed leaves

☹ Springtails.

☺ Common in warm weather in late spring and early summer. Spray emerging seedlings with MALDISON.

4 Brown spots on leaves, leaf veins become black

☹ Anthracnose.

☺ Do not plant beans for at least two years in an area where the disease has occurred. Remove diseased plants and destroy. Spray with CHAMPION COPPER.

1 **Undersides of leaves covered with tiny white insects which fly when disturbed**

☹ Whitefly.

☺ Spray with TARGET or NATURE'S WAY INSECT SPRAY at first sign and then at regular intervals to eliminate the adults as they appear. CONFIDOR also gives very effective control.

2 **Leaves yellow (stippled or mottled) becoming dehydrated. Fine webbing present on undersides of leaves**

☹ Mites.

☺ Spray with MITE KILLER, GARDEN MASTER or NATURE'S WAY INSECT SPRAY.

3 **Leaves, stems and pods develop soft, rotting areas with dusty grey mould**

☹ Botrytis, grey mould.

☺ Prevalent in wet seasons in poorly drained soils. Remove dead leaves and affected parts. Spray with GREENGUARD.

4 **Cupping and twisting of leaves**

☹ Virus.

☺ Destroy infected plants. Control insects. Plant resistant varieties, e.g. 'Tendergreen', 'Topcrop' and 'Longjohn'.

5 **Leaves, stems and pods develop soft, rotting areas with white mould containing black specks**

☹ Sclerotinia.

☺ Worse in cool, humid conditions. Space plants as far apart as possible. Remove weeds. Improve drainage. Remove diseased plants. Practise crop rotation or sterilise soil with BASAMID. Spray with GREENGUARD.

6 **Irregularly shaped lesions, often surrounded by a lighter coloured area or halo. Plants are dwarfed**

☹ Halo blight, grease spot.

☺ Wind and rain spread disease quickly. Remove and burn diseased plants at end of season. Practise crop rotation. Spray with CHAMPION COPPER or GARDEN MASTER.

1 Flowers not setting

☹ Very hot and/or windy conditions. Lack of moisture. Excess nitrogen.

☺ Plant to avoid flowers setting in mid summer. Water regularly. Use a balanced fertiliser, e.g. GRO-PLUS COMPLETE PLANT FOOD.

Poor, unthrifty growth and poor seed germination

☹ Cold.

☺ Plant to avoid frost and cold weather.

BEETROOT

2 Yellow patches between veins in leaves. Leaves brown and edges roll inwards

☹ Manganese deficiency.

☺ Do not overlime. Apply GRO-PLUS TRACE ELEMENT MIX or THRIVE ALL PURPOSE.

3 Death of young leaves. Scorched, wilted older leaves. Root flesh has blackened patches

☹ Boron deficiency.

☺ Do not overlime. Apply GRO-PLUS TRACE ELEMENT MIX or THRIVE ALL PURPOSE.

Bolting, running to seed prematurely

☹ A cold snap (below 10–15°C) followed by a warm spell.

☺ Plant slow-bolting varieties, e.g. 'Early Wonder'.

White rings, poor colour and texture in roots

☹ Root has overmatured.

☺ Harvest when young.

Poor flavour, roots lacking sweetness

☹ Excess nitrogen.

☺ Use a balanced fertiliser, e.g. GRO-PLUS COMPLETE PLANT FOOD.

Uneven growth
☹ Irregular watering.
☺ Water regularly through dry periods.

1 Light grey spots on older leaves, spreading to other parts of plant
☹ Leaf spot.
☺ More prevalent in warm wet weather. Crop rotation is important. Grow in a different position each year. Spray with CHAMPION COPPER or GARDEN MASTER.

2 Thin meandering lines through leaves
☹ Leafminer.
☺ Spray with GARDEN MASTER or CARBARYL.

Bleeding when harvesting roots
☹ Top cut too close to crown.
☺ Twist or cut tops 3 cm from crown.

3 Rusty brown spots on older leaves, which spread to younger leaves
☹ Rust.
☺ Remove diseased leaves and destroy. Spray with GARDEN MASTER.

BRASSICA (BORECOLE, BROCCOLI, BRUSSELS SPROUT, CABBAGE, CAULIFLOWER, SWEDE, TURNIP)

4 Small insects clustered in the developing heart or crown
☹ Aphids.
☺ Keep plants well watered in dry weather. Spray with TARGET, DERRIS DUST or NATURE'S WAY INSECT SPRAY.

5 Holes in leaves or stems in winter and spring
☹ Slugs and snails.
☺ Lay BLITZEM (pellets or granules) or MESUROL. Take particular care to protect seedlings.

1 Holes in leaves in late spring, summer and autumn

☹ White butterfly and diamondback moth caterpillars.

☺ Protect young plants, rather than older ones. Spray with TARGET or use DERRIS DUST.

2 Undersides of leaves covered with tiny white insects which fly when disturbed

☹ Whitefly.

☺ Spray with TARGET or NATURE'S WAY INSECT SPRAY at first sign of infection, then at regular intervals to eliminate adults.

3 Pale, pitted spots or blotches on leaves. Sometimes downy mould on undersides of leaves

☹ Downy mildew.

☺ Space plants to allow good air circulation. Spray with BRAVO, CHAMPION COPPER or GREENGUARD.

4 Scorching or burning around leaf margins. Soft and poor quality hearts. Cabbages bluish-green colour

☹ Potassium deficiency.

☺ Prevalent in sandy soils. Use balanced fertiliser, e.g. GRO-PLUS COMPLETE PLANT FOOD, THRIVE FLOWER AND FRUIT or SULPHATE OF POTASH.

5 Circular infections develop on lower outer leaves and cause premature leaf drop

☹ Cabbage ring spot.

☺ Practise crop rotation. Remove and burn infected plants. Spray with BRAVO or CHAMPION COPPER.

6 Plants stunted with deformed roots

☹ Club root.

☺ Lime the soil. Ensure good drainage. Destroy diseased plants. Practise plant rotation or sterilise soil with BASAMID. Drench seedlings in GREENGUARD before transplanting.

1 Yellowing between veins on older leaves

☹ Magnesium deficiency.

☺ Use fertiliser containing magnesium, e.g. THRIVE ALL PURPOSE, Epsom salts or dolomite lime.

2 'Whiptail' leaves, thin and straplike. Plant growth is poor

☹ Molybdenum deficiency.

☺ Apply GRO-PLUS TRACE ELEMENT MIX or THRIVE ALL PURPOSE. Molybdenum unavailable in very acidic soils — apply lime.

Heartless cabbages

☹ Too little organic matter. Soil too loose when planting. Drought.

☺ Pay attention to soil cultivation and watering.

3 Split-headed cabbages

☹ Rain after dry period. Frost.

☺ Water regularly during dry weather. Use frost protection cloth.

4 Loose, fluffy Brussels sprouts

☹ Excess nitrogen in soil. Soil too loose.

☺ Avoid nitrogenous fertilisers and excessive cultivation of soil.

5 Tiny heads on cauliflower or broccoli

☹ Cold weather.

☺ Choose all-year round varieties.

Bolting, running prematurely to seed without forming hearts

☹ Cold weather followed by warm spell or a check in growth, i.e. drought, root exposure.

☺ Use slow-bolting varieties. Check suitability of variety for the particular time of year.

6 Discoloured, yellowish cauliflower curds

☹ Direct sunlight or frost.

☺ Protect curds by folding leaves inwards or, with long-leaf varieties, tie the leaves together in the centre. Plant self-protecting varieties, e.g. 'Phenomenal 4-month Cauliflower'.

Cauliflower curds are soft and fuzzy and begin to break up

☹ Overmature.

☺ Harvest when young.

1 Hollow stems, browning or lumpiness of cauliflower

☹ Boron deficiency.

☺ Do not overlime. Apply GRO-PLUS TRACE ELEMENT MIX or THRIVE ALL PURPOSE.

2 Browning or brown streaks in flesh of turnips with water-soaked cracks. Bitter taste

☹ Boron deficiency.

☺ Apply GRO-PLUS TRACE ELEMENT MIX to soil before planting.

3 Split roots of turnips

☹ Irregular growth from uneven watering.

☺ Water regularly through dry weather.

Turnip roots coarse and stringy

☹ Overmaturity.

☺ Harvest when young and tender.

BROAD BEAN

4 Young growing tips deformed with clusters of insects

☹ Aphids.

☺ Keep plants watered in dry weather. Spray with TARGET or NATURE'S WAY INSECT SPRAY at first sign of infestation.

5 Dark brown or black spots on leaves

☹ Chocolate spot, botrytis.

☺ Spray with GREENGUARD. Good drainage helps avoid the problem. Space plants to encourage good air circulation. Control weeds.

1   Red or purple raised rust pustules, particularly on undersides of leaves

☹ Rust.

☺ Spray with BRAVO at first sign of infection.

Distorted leaves and pods

☹ Green vegetable bug.

☺ Spray with MAVRIK. Insecticides with stronger odour can be detected by the green vegetable bug, which will fly away before the sprays can be effective, only to reinfest the plant later.

Poor fruit set

☹ Too cold at flowering — planted too early.

☺ Plant later to ensure warmer temperatures at fruit set.

CARROT and PARSNIP

2   Leaves are stunted and deformed with clusters of insects

☹ Aphids.

☺ Keep well watered in dry weather. Spray with NATURE'S WAY INSECT SPRAY or PYRETHRUM.

3   Carrots tunnelled by grubs. Leaves may turn orange

☹ Carrot rust fly.

☺ Place SOIL INSECT KILLER granules in seed row when sowing. Rotate crops.

4   Forked and misshapen roots

☹ Stones, clods or lumps of bulky organic manure in soil. Delayed thinning.

☺ Prepare a deep, crumbly, well-drained soil which allows roots to expand and grow quickly. Thin   to 2–3 cm apart when carrots are 5 cm high.

Seedlings burn off

☹ Hot sunny weather at tender stage of growth.

☺ Sprinkle with water to keep moist.

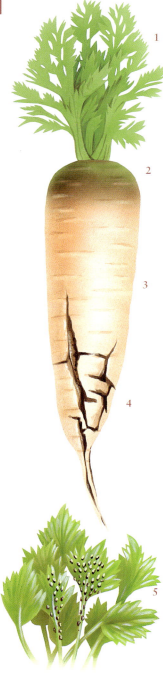

1 Excessive leaf growth

☹ Excess nitrogen.

☺ Avoid nitrogenous fertilisers. Use a balanced fertiliser, e.g. GRO-PLUS COMPLETE PLANT FOOD.

2 Green tops of carrot roots

☹ Sunlight on exposed crowns.

☺ Earth up to cover crowns during growth.

3 Carrots pale colour

☹ Pale variety e.g. 'Egmont Gold'. Strongly acid soil. Excess nitrogen.

☺ Plant deeply coloured varieties, e.g. 'Chatanay Red Core' or 'Manchester Table'. Lime the soil. Avoid nitrogen fertiliser. Potash increases intensity of colour.

4 Roots cracked or split

☹ Interior grows faster than skin, caused by heavy rain following a dry spell or overfertilising.

☺ Water frequently during dry weather.

Bolting or running to seed prematurely without forming roots

☹ Seedlings subject to snap of cool weather.

☺ Cover with cloche if cold snap forecast.

Poor parsnip germination

☹ Seed is short-lived.

☺ Use fresh parsnip seed each year.

CELERY

5 Clusters of insects on leaves, particularly in the young crown area

☹ Aphids.

☺ Keep well watered in dry weather. Spray with NATURE'S WAY INSECT SPRAY, PYRETHRUM or MALDISON.

1 Leaves covered with small black spots, or brown rusty spots on leaves and stems

☹ Septoria leaf spot.

☺ Most prevalent in cool weather. Use disease-free seed. Practise crop rotation on a 7-year cycle. Spray with BRAVO or CHAMPION COPPER.

Bolting or running prematurely to seed

☹ Cold snap followed by a warm spell. Soil drying out.

☺ Water regularly during dry weather.

2 Thin, dry stalks

☹ Lack of fertiliser and/or moisture.

☺ Feed and water regularly.

3 Split stalks

☹ Dry soil. Excess nitrogen in soil.

☺ Water thoroughly in dry weather. Use a balanced fertiliser, e.g. GRO-PLUS COMPETE PLANT FOOD.

CHIVES

4 Small black insects feeding on leaves

☹ Aphids.

☺ Keep well watered in dry weather. Spray with NATURE'S WAY INSECT SPRAY, PYRETHRUM or MALDISON.

CUCURBIT (COURGETTE, CUCUMBER, ROCK MELON, MARROW, MELON, PUMPKIN, WATERMELON, ZUCCHINI)

5 Undersides of leaves covered with tiny white insects, which fly when disturbed

☹ Whitefly.

☺ Control is difficult once a large population has built up. Spray with TARGET, CONFIDOR or NATURE'S WAY INSECT SPRAY at first sign of infestation, then regularly.

1 Leaves yellow (stippled or mottled), becoming dehydrated. Fine webbing present on undersides of leaves

☹ Mites.

☺ Most severe in warm weather. Spray with MITE KILLER, NATURE'S WAY INSECT SPRAY or GARDEN MASTER.

2 Flowers and fruit rot in humid conditions

☹ Botrytis, grey mould.

☺ Prevalent in humid conditions. Spray with BRAVO.

3 Leaves become blotched and yellow, sometimes with mould on undersides

☹ Downy mildew.

☺ In cool, moist conditions an attack can be severe. Spray with BRAVO or NATURE'S WAY FUNGUS SPRAY.

4 White or grey mould on leaves, starting as spots and spreading over the whole leaf

☹ Powdery mildew.

☺ Most common in warm dry conditions. Spray with NATURE'S WAY FUNGUS SPRAY, GREENGUARD or GARDEN MASTER.

5 Wilting of leaves

☹ Large leaves lose moisture quickly in warm weather.

☺ Water frequently and thoroughly. Mulch around plants to conserve soil moisture.

Excessive leaf growth

☹ Excess nitrogen.

☺ Use a balanced fertiliser, e.g. GRO-PLUS COMPLETE PLANT FOOD.

Fruit yellow and bitter to taste

☹ Overmaturity.

☺ Harvest when young.

1 Water-soaked spots on leaves which dry and crack. Immature fruit may fall

☹ Leaf spot.

☺ Crop rotation of two years or more is important. Destroy diseased material. Spray with BRAVO or CHAMPION COPPER.

2 Brown-black spots on leaves

☹ Anthracnose.

☺ Do not grow cucurbits in the same soil more than once in every four years. Spray with CHAMPION COPPER or GARDEN MASTER.

Shortage of fruit

☹ Poor pollination caused by absence of bees in dull, cold weather.

☺ Fruit setting improves with warmer weather. Hand pollinate. To keep plants cropping it is necessary to remove fruit as they mature.

3 Predominance of male flowers.

☹ Under certain stress conditions (poor nutrition, low light, low temperatures, low water) the male flowers of some cultivars become dominant on the plant.

☺ Ensure plants receive adequate nutrition and appropriate water.

4 Damaged skin with pale, discoloured blotches

☹ Fruit exposed to wet, damp soil.

☺ Place block of wood or tile under fruits to keep them off damp soil.

Lack of flavour

☹ Harvested before fully ripened.

☺ To test for ripeness:

Watermelon: Skin becomes slightly bumpy on side of fruit in contact with soil.

Rock melon: Stalk comes away from fruit. Fruit develops flavour if kept for two or three days.

EGGPLANT (AUBERGINE)

1 Small insects on new growth. Leaves wilt and twist

☹ Aphids.

☺ Keep plants well watered in dry weather. Spray at first sign of infection with MALDISON or NATURE'S WAY INSECT SPRAY.

2 Distortion of young leaves and silvering of older leaves

☹ Thrips.

☺ Spray at first sign with CARBARYL, CONFIDOR or MALDISON.

3 Leaves chewed

☹ Caterpillars.

☺ Spray with CARBARYL, PYRETHRUM or GARDEN MASTER to control caterpillars. Alternatively, pick off insects by hand.

4 Plants wilt and die rapidly

☹ Sclerotinia.

☺ Destroy infected plants. Avoid fluctuations in watering. Spray with GREENGUARD as a preventative measure.

5 Streaks in foliage

☹ Virus.

☺ Destroy infected plants. Control aphids and thrips to prevent infection. Plant resistant varieties, e.g. 'Blacknite' and 'Blackbell'.

Poor fruit set

☹ Lack of pollination.

☺ Cool, dull weather and lack of insects. May require hand pollination with a small brush.

KUMARA

1 Galls on roots. Poor growth

🙁 Nematodes.

🙂 Rotate crop so kumaras are not grown in the same area more than one year in three. Alternatively, sterilise soil with BASAMID granules.

LETTUCE

2 Insects clustered on leaves

🙁 Aphids.

🙂 More common in dry weather. Keep plants well watered. Spray with NATURE'S WAY INSECT SPRAY, MALDISON or PYRETHRUM.

3 Brown spots on leaves

🙁 Leaf spot.

🙂 Common after cold, wet weather in badly drained situations. Practise crop rotation. Spray with GARDEN MASTER or COPPER OXYCHLORIDE.

4 Soft rot of leaves with grey mould

🙁 Botrytis, grey mould.

🙂 Prevalent in humid weather. Spreads rapidly. Improve drainage. Spray with GARDEN MASTER or BRAVO.

5 Stunting, rotting at ground level; brown slime rot in hearts. Bitterness

🙁 Sclerotinia.

🙂 Remove affected plants with surrounding soil and destroy. Spray healthy plants with GREENGUARD.

Bolting, running to seed prematurely

🙁 Check in growth, i.e. delayed transplanting, overcrowding, dryness, hot weather.

🙂 Select right variety for growing in summer and winter. Pay particular attention to soil preparation, watering, and feeding.

Bitterness

☹ Slow growth and/or overmaturity.

☺ Grow quickly in warm soils with plenty of moisture.

Poor seed germination

☹ Lack of moisture. Too hot.

☺ At 20°C, germination takes 7–10 days. Above 25°C seeds become dormant. Use fresh seed.

Young seedlings eaten

☹ Slugs or snails.

☺ Protect with BLITZEM or MESUROL.

1 No hearts

☹ Shortage of organic matter. Not enough light. Overcrowding. Drought.

☺ Incorporate organic matter into soil at planting time, e.g. compost or BIO-GOLD ORGANIC FERTILISER. Space plants and keep them watered.

2 'Tipburn', leaf edges turn brown

☹ Sudden water loss from leaves during warm spell.

☺ Ensure even watering in warm conditions.

ONION (GARLIC, LEEK, SHALLOT)

3 Foliage blotched, silver, grey or white, leaves becoming deformed in severe cases

☹ Thrips.

☺ Most common in dry weather. Control weeds and keep plants well watered. Spray with MAVRIK.

4 Grey or purple spots on leaves. Pitted appearance

☹ Downy mildew.

☺ More serious in wet weather. Improve soil drainage and air circulation. Spray with GARDEN MASTER or NATURE'S WAY FUNGUS SPRAY.

1 Heavy top growth and drooping leaves

☹ Too much fresh manure or nitrogen in soil.

☺ Work organic matter into the soil thoroughly. Use a balanced fertiliser, e.g. GRO-PLUS COMPLETE PLANT FOOD.

Soft bulbs

☹ Excess nitrogen.

☺ Use balanced fertiliser, e.g. GRO-PLUS COMPLETE PLANT FOOD.

Poor keeping quality

☹ Excessive moisture.

☺ Plant long-keeping variety, e.g. 'Pukekohe Longkeeper'.

2 Thick necks in mature onions

☹ Delay in transplanting of seedling. Sowing too early. Excess nitrogen. Planting too deep. Dry soil in early growth period.

☺ Transplant before seedling stem exceeds 6 mm in width. Use balanced fertiliser, e.g. GRO-PLUS COMPLETE PLANT FOOD. Water regularly in dry weather.

3 Soft rots with grey or brown mould. Common in storage

☹ Botrytis, grey mould.

☺ Spray with GARDEN MASTER. Store in dry, well-ventilated conditions.

Failing to bulb

☹ Sowing too late. Excess nitrogen.

☺ Sow seed June to July. Use balanced fertiliser, e.g. GRO-PLUS COMPLETE PLANT FOOD.

4 Bulbs split at base

☹ Heavy rain or watering after a prolonged dry spell.

☺ Water frequently during dry weather.

Bolting, plant runs to seed

☹ Seed sown too early.

☺ Sow seed in June to July.

PARSLEY

1   **Wilting of plant. Leaves puckered and distorted. Insects under leaves or on new growth**

☹ Aphids.

☺ Water regularly in dry weather. Spray with NATURE'S WAY INSECT SPRAY or PYRETHRUM.

2   **Silvering of leaves**

☹ Thrips.

☺ Spray with CARBARYL.

3   **Spots on leaves**

☹ Leaf spot.

☺ Cut and destroy infected parts. Spray with CHAMPION COPPER or NATURE'S WAY FUNGUS SPRAY.

PEA

4   **Wilting of plant. Leaves puckered and distorted. Insects under leaves or on new growth**

☹ Aphids.

☺ Water regularly in dry weather. Spray with MALDISON, GARDEN MASTER, NATURE'S WAY INSECT SPRAY or PYRETHRUM.

5   **Leaf surfaces yellow or pitted with grey mould on undersides**

☹ Downy mildew.

☺ Avoid areas with shade or poor air circulation. Spray with CHAMPION COPPER or NATURE'S WAY FUNGUS SPRAY.

6   **Irregular, dark, water-soaked spots or lesions. Young infected pods shrivel**

☹ Bacterial blight.

☺ More prevalent in cool, damp weather. Spray with CHAMPION COPPER or NATURE'S WAY FUNGUS SPRAY. Practise a three-year crop rotation.

Flowers not setting

☹ Frosty conditions.

☺ Plant to avoid frosts.

1 Plants stunted and yellow

☹ Wet soil, poor drainage. Lack of fertiliser.

☺ Improve soil conditions and apply a balanced fertiliser, e.g. GRO-PLUS COMPLETE PLANT FOOD.

PEPPER (CAPSICUM)

2 Plant wilts, leaves pucker and distort. Insects under leaves or on new growth

☹ Aphids.

☺ Water regularly. Spray with NATURE'S WAY INSECT SPRAY, PYRETHRUM or MALDISON.

3 Leaves become silvery and dehydrated with brown specks on undersides

☹ Thrips.

☺ Spray with MALDISON or CARBARYL.

4 Soft, brown rot which develops a white, fluffy growth

☹ Sclerotinia.

☺ Disease is worse in cool, humid conditions. Practise crop rotation and improve drainage. Sterilise soil with BASAMID.

5 Streaking of foliage

☹ Virus.

☺ Control aphids and thrips throughout growing season. Destroy virus-infected plants. Plant resistant varieties, e.g. 'Yates Wonder' and 'Californian Wonder'.

POTATO

6 Plant wilts, leaves pucker and distort. Insects under leaves or on new growth

☹ Aphids.

☺ Keep well watered in dry weather. Spray with PYRETHRUM, ORTHENE, MALDISON or NATURE'S WAY INSECT SPRAY.

1 Blotches and holes in leaves. Tunnels in stems and tubers

☹ Potato tuber moth.

☺ Incorporate plenty of organic matter in soil and keep plants well watered. Spray with CARBARYL, GARDEN MASTER or ORTHENE.

2 Irregular, greenish brown-black patches on leaves and stalks, rapidly enlarging in wet weather. Whole plant becomes blackened

☹ Late blight.

☺ Most common in humid conditions with cool nights and warm days. Spray regularly with BRAVO, CHAMPION COPPER, GREENGUARD or GARDEN MASTER.

3 Small spots on older leaves, increasing to 1 cm in size. Concentric rings can be seen in the spot

☹ Early blight.

☺ Common in hot, humid weather. Spray with BRAVO, CHAMPION COPPER or GARDEN MASTER.

4 Yellow, blotched leaves

☹ Late spring frosts damage shoots.

☺ Plant to avoid frosts.

No sprouts on seed tubers

☹ Frosting of seed tubers in transit or in storage. Diseased tuber.

☺ Keep tubers cool, but do not freeze.

Soft and rubbery tubers

☹ Dry summer.

☺ Water frequently during dry spells.

5 Spindly sprouts on seed tubers

☹ Keeping tubers too dark or too warm prior to planting.

☺ Store seed tubers in well-ventilated, cool position in indirect light.

1 Yellowing and browning of tissue between the veins of leaflets

☹ Magnesium deficiency.

☺ Apply fertiliser containing magnesium when preparing the soil for planting, e.g. GRO-PLUS COMPLETE PLANT FOOD or add Epsom salts.

2 Yellow mottling on leaves. Crinkling of leaf tissue. Plants may die early

☹ Mosaic virus.

☺ Plant only certified seed. Control aphids.

Tubers crack and split during growth

☹ Tubers suffered dry spell.

☺ Keep well watered.

Tubers with soapy, waxy texture

☹ Lifting tubers before mature. Excess lime.

☺ For storing potatoes, dig after the top has completely died down. Only apply lime to acidic soils.

3 Hollow centres in large tubers

☹ Prolonged wet spell after dry weather.

☺ Keep watered during dry weather.

Tubers with sweet taste

☹ Tubers too cool in storage.

☺ Store in a cool, dark place.

4 Tubers have black heart or turn black when cooked

☹ Potash deficiency. Stored in too high temperatures (above 10°C).

☺ Use a balanced fertiliser, e.g. GRO-PLUS COMPLETE PLANT FOOD. Store in a cool place.

Poor emergence and/or small tubers

☹ Sweating of tubers in storage caused by poor ventilation. Tubers stored for over six months.

☺ Store carefully. Do not plant too late. Avoid planting in cold, wet soil.

RADISH, SWEDE and TURNIP

1 Wilting of plant. Leaves puckered and distorted. Insects under leaves or on new growth

- ☹ Aphids.
- ☺ Keep well watered during dry weather. Spray with MALDISON, PYRETHRUM, NATURE'S WAY INSECT SPRAY or GARDEN MASTER.

2 Holes in leaves

- ☹ Caterpillars.
- ☺ Spray with CARBARYL, PYRETHRUM or GARDEN MASTER.

3 Irregular, black patches on root

- ☹ Black root.
- ☺ More common in warm weather and if soil is moist. Improve soil drainage. Practise crop rotation.

4 Deformed roots

- ☹ Club root.
- ☺ Lime the soil. Ensure good drainage. Do not grow more than once in seven years in the same area, or sterilise soil with BASAMID. Drench seedlings in GREENGUARD.

SILVERBEET

Seedlings eaten

- ☹ Slugs or snails.
- ☺ Protect with BLITZEM or MESUROL.

5 Fine tracings appear on leaves

- ☹ Silverbeet leafminer.
- ☺ Spray with CARBARYL or MALDISON.

6 Red-brown pustules form on leaves

- ☹ Rust.
- ☺ Spray with GARDEN MASTER.

1 Chewed foliage

☹ Caterpillars.

☺ Spray with CARBARYL or GARDEN MASTER and apply DERRIS DUST.

Bolting, running to seed prematurely

☹ Prolonged cold spell followed by warm weather. Transplanting shock.

☺ Sow seed directly into the ground where possible, to avoid transplanting shock.

SPINACH

Bolting, running to seed prematurely

☹ Long days and high temperatures. Check in growth. Lack of water or fertiliser. Overcrowding.

☺ Do not overcrowd plants. Keep well watered in dry weather.

2 Yellow blotches between veins in leaves

☹ Manganese deficiency (common in sandy soils) or soil too alkaline.

☺ Do not overlime. Apply GRO-PLUS TRACE ELEMENT MIX. Foliar feed with THRIVE ALL PURPOSE or LUSH ALL PURPOSE.

SWEET CORN

3 Leaves eaten, tassel eaten and cobs attacked

☹ Army caterpillar.

☺ Spray with CARBARYL or MALDISON.

Galls form on cob

☹ Smut.

☺ Destroy infected plants. Use clean seed.

Tough kernels

☹ Overmature when harvested. Storing cobs too long. Overcooking.

☺ Pick and use cobs when young and fresh. Use new 'Super Sweet' varieties.

1 Poorly filled cobs

☹ Poor pollination.

☺ Plant in blocks rather than rows.

Corn eaten at end of cob

☹ Corn ear worm.

☺ Control when plants are young. Spray with CARBARYL or MALDISON.

TOMATO

2 Split fruit

☹ Heavy watering or rain when temperatures are high.

☺ Water regularly through dry periods.

Blossom drop

☹ Low temperatures in spring or very high temperatures in summer.

☺ Grow a variety suited to the season, e.g. 'Early Money' for early or late crops. Protect plants from wind.

3 Paper-brown patches on fruit

☹ Sun scald, exposure to bright sunlight.

☺ Do not remove too many old leaves at once. Shade plants.

4 Bottom of fruit sunken, leathery and blackened

☹ Blossom end rot, lack of calcium, together with irregular watering.

☺ Most serious when plants are growing rapidly. Apply lime prior to planting. Water daily. Mulch plants to avoid fluctuations in soil temperature and moisture. Foliar-feed with LUSH TOMATO FOOD to supply calcium.

5 Blotchy ripening, parts of fruit remain yellow or orange

☹ Too much heat. Too little potash. Too much water.

☺ Water moderately. Feed with GRO-PLUS TOMATO FERTILISER or LUSH TOMATO FOOD.

1 Misshapen fruit

☹ Virus disease. Poor pollination due to cold weather at flowering or very high temperatures.

☺ Plant later in spring.

2 Small caterpillar tunnel holes in fruit

☹ Tomato fruit worm.

☺ Spray young plants with MAVRIK or LIQUID TOMATO SPRAY.

3 Green back, area around stalk remains hard, green and unripe

☹ Excess sunlight. Too dry. Too much potash.

☺ Apply sulphate of ammonia. Water regularly.

4 Leaves yellow between veins

☹ Magnesium deficiency.

☺ Feed with GRO-PLUS TOMATO FOOD at planting. Foliar feed with LUSH TOMATO FOOD.

5 Tiny white insects on undersides of leaves, which fly when disturbed

☹ Whitefly.

☺ Spray with TARGET, CONFIDOR, MAVRIK or NATURE'S WAY INSECT SPRAY.

6 Leaves yellow (mottled) and dehydrate in hot, dry weather, especially in glasshouses. Minute insects under leaves

☹ Mites.

☺ Spray with MITE KILLER, MAVRIK or NATURE'S WAY INSECT SPRAY.

7 Rolling of older leaves

☹ Excess deleafing or a wide variation between day and night temperatures.

☺ Mulch plants to control temperature and soil moisture fluctuations.

8 Plant wilts, leaves pucker and distort. Insects under leaves or on new growth

☹ Aphids.

☺ Spray with TARGET, MAVRIK, CONFIDOR or LIQUID TOMATO SPRAY.

1 Small spots on older leaves. Dark mould present

☹ Early blight.

☺ More common in warm, wet weather. Prevent by spraying regularly with CHAMPION COPPER, BRAVO or TOMATO SPRAY. Remove affected plants.

2 Irregular, brown patches on leaves, spreading rapidly in wet weather

☹ Late blight.

☺ Serious in cool, humid weather. Prevent by spraying regularly with CHAMPION COPPER, BRAVO, GREENGUARD or TOMATO SPRAY. Remove affected plants.

3 Leaves, stems and fruit develop a grey-brown rot or mould

☹ Botrytis, grey mould.

☺ Spray with BRAVO, LIQUID TOMATO SPRAY or GREENGUARD.

4 Older leaves showing yellow blotches with grey mould on undersides. Young leaves showing pale circular spots

☹ Leaf mould.

☺ Spray with BRAVO.

5 Black specks on leaves, often with a yellowish halo. Common in early spring or in cool, wet weather

☹ Bacterial spot.

☺ Use disease-free seed. Practise four to five-year crop rotation. Control weeds. Burn diseased plants. Avoid overhead watering. Spray with CHAMPION COPPER or TOMATO SPRAY.

6 Drying and withering of leaves

☹ Verticillium wilt, bacterial wilt.

☺ Do not grow in same area more than one year in three. Sterilise soil with BASAMID granules. Plant verticillium-resistant varieties, e.g. 'Bigbeef', 'Grosse Lisse' and 'Roma'.

1   **Plants suddenly stop growing. Bronze spots develop between leaves. Fruit ripens unevenly with blotches**

☹ Spotted wilt virus.

☺ Remove infected plants and destroy. Spray healthy plants with CONFIDOR for thrips control.

2   **Yellowing of leaves at base of plant. Stems show brown discolouration if cut**

☹ Fusarium wilt.

☺ Prevalent in warm weather. Sterilise soil with BASAMID. Plant resistant varieties, e.g. 'Summer Taste', 'Big Beef' and 'Roma'.

FRUIT

BLUEBERRY

1 Leaves rolled, folded and chewed

☹ Leaf roller caterpillar.

☺ Spray with CARBARYL or GARDEN MASTER. Organic control can be achieved by hanging sticky yellow caterpillar traps on the plant.

2 Chewed leaf edges in November and December. Defoliation of some plants

☹ Grass grub beetle.

☺ Spray with CARBARYL or MALDISON in November and December.

3 Notches and holes chewed out of leaves. Dieback of plants

☹ Weevils.

☺ Spray with CARBARYL or MALDISON.

4 Wilting of plant. Large numbers of insects which jump when disturbed

☹ Passion vine hopper.

☺ Spray with PYRETHRUM, MAVRIK or MALDISON. The adult passion vine hopper is very difficult to eradicate. Control is best achieved by spraying when the insects are in their juvenile stage, characterised by their fluffy white tail.

5 Black sooty mould on leaves and stems

☹ Sooty mould.

☺ Sooty mould lives on honeydew secreted from mealybugs. Spray with MALDISON or CARBARYL.

6 Wilting of plant. Leaves distorted and puckered. Insects under leaves or on new growth

☹ Aphids.

☺ Spray with PYRETHRUM or MALDISON.

1 Wilting of leaves and dieback of twigs

☹ Scale.

☺ Spray with MALDISON and CONQUEROR OIL.

2 Stunting of plants. Galls on roots

☹ Nematodes.

☺ Remove infected plants. Sterilise soil with BASAMID granules.

BRAMBLE (BLACKBERRY, BOYSENBERRY, DEWBERRY, LOGANBERRY) (see also Raspberry)

3 Buds eaten and leaves emerge in tatters

☹ Raspberry bud moth.

☺ Prune as soon after picking as possible. Spray with CARBARYL or MALDISON through growing season.

4 Hole in stem end of fruit. Grubs in fruit. Leaves rolled together

☹ Leaf roller caterpillar.

☺ Spray with CARBARYL or MALDISON.

5 Leaves become stippled, yellow and dehydrated. Fine webbing is sometimes visible on underside of leaves

☹ Mites.

☺ Common in hot, dry weather. Spray with NATURE'S WAY INSECT SPRAY, MAVRIK or MITE KILLER.

6 Leaves have purple or black patches. Stems develop purple patches. Fruit is deformed and shrivelled

☹ Dry berry, downy mildew.

☺ Spray with BRAVO.

7 Fruit develops a grey mould, becomes soft, watery and rots

☹ Botrytis, grey mould.

☺ Spray with BRAVO, particularly during flowering if rain is expected.

CITRUS (GRAPEFRUIT, LEMON, MANDARIN, ORANGE, TANGELO)

1 **Clusters of black insects on young leaves**

☹ Aphids.

☺ Keep plants well watered in dry weather. Spray with ORTHENE, CONFIDOR or TARGET.

2 **Presence of black, sooty mould. Small, mealy insects found in protected cavities**

☹ Mealybug.

☺ Spray with ORTHENE, CONFIDOR or TARGET.

3 **Poor growth, pale dehydrated leaves. Fruit small and dry. Hard, scale-like insects on woody and green stems**

☹ Scale.

☺ Scale numbers quickly build up in dry seasons. Spray with ORTHENE, CONFIDOR and CONQUEROR OIL over the summer.

4 **Leaves tightly rolled and foliage and surface fruit eaten**

☹ Leaf roller caterpillar.

☺ Spray with ORTHENE, TARGET from October to March.

5 **Snow white, soft scale. Sooty mould present**

☹ Soft wax scale.

☺ Spray with CONQUEROR OIL and CONFIDOR or ORTHENE.

6 **Silvering of foliage and fruit. Black spots of excrement may be seen**

☹ Thrips.

☺ Spray with CONFIDOR, ORTHENE or MALDISON from November to March.

1 **Leaves yellow and dehydrated. Minute insects under leaves**

☹ Mites.

☺ Common in hot, dry weather. Spray with MAVRIK or MITE KILLER.

2 **Trees show poor growth, are dehydrated and branches die. Holes in branches and presence of 'sawdust'**

☹ Lemon tree borer.

☺ Prune out infected wood and burn. Spray with ORTHENE when not in fruit or inject MALDISON into holes.

3 **Fruit develops brown rot and drops from the tree. The disease has a characteristic smell**

☹ Citrus brown rot.

☺ Prune out the lower branches of tree to increase air circulation. Spray with CHAMPION COPPER.

4 **Splits and puckers in leaves**

☹ Wind damage causing new leaves to rub against branches or thorns.

☺ Shelter from strong winds.

5 **Pale, small leaves**

☹ Lack of fertiliser.

☺ Citrus are heavy feeders. Feed in spring and autumn with GRO-PLUS CITRUS FOOD.

6 **Light green leaves fading to pale yellow or white. Veins remain green**

☹ Iron deficiency.

☺ Common in alkaline soils. Fertilise with GRO-PLUS CITRUS FOOD or GRO-PLUS IRON SULPHATE.

7 **Irregular, grey, scabby, wart-like growth on fruit or stems**

☹ Verrucosis, scab.

☺ Spray with CHAMPION COPPER or COPPER OXYCHLORIDE.

1 New leaves small and narrow, growing close together

☹ Zinc deficiency.

☺ Spray foliage with LUSH ALL PURPOSE or THRIVE ALL PURPOSE. Apply GRO-PLUS TRACE ELEMENT MIX. Zinc is leached out of light, sandy soils and may be unavailable in highly alkaline soils.

2 Spots on leaves, fruit and stems of mandarins

☹ Brown spot.

☺ Common in cool, damp weather. Prune dead material and burn it. Spray with CHAMPION COPPER.

3 Older leaves yellow from outer edge

☹ Magnesium deficiency.

☺ More common in acid soils. Spray foliage with LUSH ALL PURPOSE or THRIVE ALL PURPOSE and fertilise regularly with GRO-PLUS CITRUS FOOD.

4 Small, dark, red-brown spots on leaves and fruit, often merging. Skin may crack

☹ Melanose.

☺ More common on older trees in warm humid weather. Prune off dead twigs and branches. Spray with CHAMPION COPPER or COPPER OXYCHLORIDE at monthly intervals.

CURRANT

Shoots and stems wilt and die due to hollowing-out by boring insect

☹ Currant borer.

☺ Remove and burn infected parts.

5 Leaves rolled together

☹ Leaf roller caterpillar.

☺ Spray with CARBARYL.

FEIJOA

1 **Poor growth. Dehydrated leaves. Hard, scale-like insects on woody and green stems**

☹ Scale.

☺ Scale numbers build up quickly in dry seasons. Spray with CONQUEROR OIL over the summer.

2 **Leaves rolled or stuck together. Surface of fruit eaten**

☹ Leaf roller caterpillar.

☺ Spray with CARBARYL or MALDISON.

3 **Leaves yellow (stippled or mottled), becoming dehydrated. Fine webbing present on undersides of leaves**

☹ Mites.

☺ Spray with MAVRIK, MITE KILLER or NATURE'S WAY INSECT SPRAY.

GOOSEBERRY

4 **Brown spots on leaves**

☹ Leaf spot.

☺ Spray with BRAVO or CHAMPION COPPER.

5 **Silver appearance of leaves. Poor growth**

☹ Silver leaf.

☺ Cut out infected wood and burn. Prune in dry weather. Seal cuts with BACSEAL PRUNING PAINT.

6 **Leaves develop a spreading white mould**

☹ Powdery mildew.

☺ Spray with GARDEN MASTER or NATURE'S WAY FUNGUS SPRAY.

GRAPE

7 **Young leaves webbed together and eaten. Fruit shrivels**

☹ Leaf roller caterpillar.

☺ Spray with TARGET, CARBARYL or FRUIT TREE SPRAY.

1   Black spots on stems and leaves

☹   Black spot.

☺   Common in cool, damp weather. Spray with BRAVO, GREENGUARD or NATURE'S WAY FUNGUS SPRAY.

2   Yellow or brown irregular spots on leaves. Brown spots on fruit. A grey-brown mould develops under leaves

☹   Downy mildew.

☺   Worst in warm or humid conditions. Avoid overhead watering. Prune to minimise shaded, moist pockets. Spray regularly with BRAVO, CHAMPION COPPER, or NATURE'S WAY FUNGUS SPRAY.

3   White, powdery film on leaves and fruit. Mouldy smell

☹   Powdery mildew.

☺   Common in warm weather. Spray with BRAVO, GREENGUARD, NATURE'S WAY FUNGUS SPRAY, FUNGUS FIGHTER or FRUIT TREE SPRAY.

4   Fruit develops a grey-brown mould and rots

☹   Botrytis, grey mould.

☺   Most prevalent in warm, wet weather late in the season. Spray with BRAVO or GREENGUARD, particularly at flowering to prevent later development.

5   Weak growth. Reduced crops. Leaves may have irregular swellings on lower surface

☹   Phylloxera aphid.

☺   Vines in heavy clay soils are more susceptible to this. Destroy infected plants. Grow grapes on resistant root stock.

6   No fruit set. Leaves turn red-brown prematurely. Stunted appearance

☹   Virus.

☺   Destroy plant.

GUAVA

1 **Fruit develop roughened areas and become hard. Leaves silver and dehydrated**

☹ Thrips.

☺ Most common in hot weather. Spray with CARBARYL or MALDISON at flowering in the evening when bees are not present.

KIWIFRUIT

2 **Leaves folded or rolled together. Fruit skin chewed**

☹ Leaf roller caterpillar.

☺ Spray with MAVRIK, CARBARYL or MALDISON.

3 **Chewed leaf edges, mostly in November and December**

☹ Grass grub beetle.

☺ Spray with CARBARYL or MALDISON.

4 **Ragged notching of leaves**

☹ Weevil.

☺ Spray with CARBARYL or MALDISON.

5 **Sticky honeydew on which sooty mould may grow**

☹ Passion vine hopper.

☺ Spray with PYRETHRUM or MALDISON.

6 **Small insects feeding on new growth, causing distortion**

☹ Aphids.

☺ Spray with PYRETHRUM or MALDISON.

7 **White fluffy insects present**

☹ Mealybug.

☺ Spray with CARBARYL, MALDISON or PYRETHRUM.

8 **Small brown scale. Plant does not thrive. Dimples on fruit. Tips of twigs die back**

☹ Scale.

☺ Spray with MALDISON.

1 Bronzing of leaves with webbing on undersides

☹ Mites.

☺ Spray with MITE KILLER or NATURE'S WAY INSECT SPRAY.

LOQUAT

Juvenile plants wilt

☹ Phytophthora root rot.

☺ Soil too wet. Plant in a free-draining soil.

2 Black spots or scabs on leaves and fruit

☹ Black spot.

☺ Select resistant strains. Spray with CHAMPION COPPER or NATURE'S WAY FUNGUS SPRAY.

3 Leaves become blackened, particularly in cool, wet weather

☹ Fire blight (bacterial disease).

☺ Remove infected wood and burn. Spray with CHAMPION COPPER or NATURE'S WAY FUNGUS SPRAY.

PASSIONFRUIT

Young plants eaten

☹ Slugs or snails.

☺ Protect with BLITZEM or MESUROL.

4 Insects in clusters on young leaves

☹ Aphids.

☺ Water regularly in dry weather. Spray with MALDISON, NATURE'S WAY INSECT SPRAY or PYRETHRUM.

5 Presence of black, sooty mould. Small, mealy insects found close to stems and protected cavities

☹ Mealybug.

☺ Spray with MALDISON or CARBARYL to control insects.

1 Leaves eaten

☺ Caterpillars.

☺ Spray with CARBARYL or PYRETHRUM.

2 Brown spots on leaves and fruit

☺ Septoria spot or brown spot.

☺ Spray with CHAMPION COPPER.

3 Small insects which jump when disturbed

☺ Passion vine hopper.

☺ Spray with MALDISON or PYRETHRUM.

4 Woodiness of fruit. Rind is very thick with small fruit cavity. Leaves maybe mottled

☺ Virus disease carried by aphids.

☺ Control insects. Replace vines every three to five years.

5 Fruit, leaves and stems develop a grey mould and rot

☺ Botrytis, grey mould.

☺ Most common in wet or humid weather. Spray with GARDEN MASTER or NATURE'S WAY FUNGUS SPRAY.

6 Brown patches on mature leaves and fruit, and shoots may die from the tips

☺ Phytophthora blight.

☺ Plant where vines receive maximum amount of sun and ensure they are well spaced.

Plants wilt, collapse and die

☺ Fusarium root rot.

☺ Plant in well drained soil. Avoid replanting in same position.

7 Raised, rough, wet or greasy lesions on fruit. Wilting and dying of stems. Fruit shrivels and falls

☺ Grease spot, bacterial spot.

☺ More common in wet weather. Spray with CHAMPION COPPER.

PERSIMMON

1 White, cottony insects
☹ Mealybug.

☺ Spray with CARBARYL or MALDISON.

2 Leaves wilt, yellow and die
☹ Phytophthora root rot.

☺ Plant only in well-drained soil. Avoid clay soils. Avoid overwatering.

3 Small brown discs attached to leaves and stems
☹ Scale.

☺ Keep plants well watered in dry weather. Spray with CONFIDOR and CONQUEROR OIL.

Fruit not forming
☹ Plant too young.

☺ Plants take seven years to yield fruit.

4 Tiny black insects feeding on underside of leaves, silvering foliage
☹ Thrips.

☺ Spray with CARBARYL or MALDISON.

PIPFRUIT (APPLE, PEAR, QUINCE)

5 Insects clustered on new growth
☹ Aphids.

☺ Spray with MALDISON or FRUIT TREE SPRAY.

6 Tightly rolled leaves on young shoots, which may be pink in colour
☹ Leaf curling midge.

☺ Damage most severe on young trees. The fly overwinters as a pupa in the soil. Application of SOIL INSECT KILLER granules under the tree in early spring will provide control. Spray foliage with MALDISON.

1 Tunnels in fruit

☹ Codling moth.

☺ Destroy infested fruit. Remove flaking bark from tree trunks. Some larvae can be trapped by placing cardboard around trunk. Hang codling moth traps from October onwards. Spray with CARBARYL from petal-fall until late harvest, at two-week intervals.

2 Leaves rolled, folded or webbed. Fruit is blemished

☹ Leaf roller caterpillar.

☺ Spray with CARBARYL, MALDISON or FRUIT TREE SPRAY.

3 Leaves become yellow (stippled or mottled) and dehydrated in hot weather. Minute insects under leaves

☹ Mites.

☺ Spray with CONQUEROR OIL in late winter to control eggs. Spray with MITE KILLER, NATURE'S WAY INSECT SPRAY or FRUIT TREE SPRAY over summer.

4 Black spots on leaves and fruit

☹ Black spot, scab.

☺ A wet-weather disease. Destroy all leaves in autumn. Spray with CHAMPION COPPER over winter. Spray regularly with FUNGUS FIGHTER or FRUIT TREE SPRAY from leaf burst.

5 New growing tips die. Gum is produced around the twig

☹ Oriental fruit moth.

☺ Cut off and burn any infested twigs 5 cm below dieback. Spray with CARBARYL, MALDISON or FRUIT TREE SPRAY.

6 Areas of dead bark cracking in rings, often completely around a branch

☹ European canker.

☺ Spray with CHAMPION COPPER at leaf fall. Remove and burn diseased wood.

1 **White, powdery mould on leaves, particularly the young growing tips. Fruit develops with yellowish criss-crossing lines on skins**

☹ Powdery mildew.

☺ Spray regularly with FUNGUS FIGHTER.

2 **Dark brown spots on ripening fruit**

☹ Glomerella or ripe spot.

☺ Collect and burn all small, distorted fruit and dead wood. Prune centre of tree to improve circulation. Spray with FRUIT TREE SPRAY.

3 **Water-soaked spots on fruit skin. Pits turn brown and become dry and spongy**

☹ Bitter pit (calcium deficiency).

☺ Occurs more on young trees. Spray foliage with LUSH TOMATO FOOD (contains calcium) early in the season. Avoid heavy pruning.

4 **Fruit cracks. Rough skin and dark, spongy areas in fruit**

☹ Boron deficiency.

☺ Avoid fluctuations in soil moisture. Spray with THRIVE ALL PURPOSE or LUSH ALL PURPOSE.

5 **Chewed leaf edges**

☹ Bronze beetle, grass grub beetle.

☺ Spray with CARBARYL, MALDISON or FRUIT TREE SPRAY.

6 **Leaves become blackened and die back**

☹ Fire blight (bacterial disease).

☺ Remove and burn infected wood. Spray with CHAMPION COPPER. Protect wounds with BACSEAL PRUNING PAINT.

7 **Yellow-green hopping insects that feed by sucking plant sap, producing white areas.**

☹ Leaf hopper.

☺ Spray with MALDISON, CARBARYL or FRUIT TREE SPRAY.

1 Leaf surface removed with only veins left (pear only)

☹ Cherry slug.

☺ Spray with CARBARYL, FRUIT TREE SPRAY or PYRETHRUM.

2 Sooty mould

☹ Mealybug insect secretes honeydew on which mould grows.

☺ Spray with CARBARYL, MALDISON or FRUIT TREE SPRAY.

3 Scarlet spotting on fruit

☹ San Jose scale.

☺ Spray with CONQUEROR OIL in winter.

Marked skin

☹ Oyster shell scale.

☺ Spray with CONQUEROR OIL in winter.

4 Lumps and scars on twigs, with white, cottony masses

☹ Woolly aphid.

☺ Spray with MALDISON.

RASPBERRY (see also Bramble)

No fruit

☹ Incorrect pruning.

☺ Remove old canes only, leave young canes intact.

5 Yellow pustules on leaves which later turn black

☹ Rust.

☺ Spray with GARDEN MASTER at first sign of infection.

6 Buds eaten out. Shoots emerge in tatters

☹ Raspberry bud moth.

☺ Prune as soon after fruiting as possible. Spray with CARBARYL over spring and summer.

1 Spots on canes and leaves. Canes may crack

☺ Cane spot.

☺ Prune out and burn infected canes. Avoid overcrowding. Spray with CHAMPION COPPER.

Wilting and dying back of cane

☺ Cane wilt.

☺ Remove and burn old fruiting canes and infected young canes. Spray with CHAMPION COPPER at green tip stage.

2 Berries hard, dry and split. Leaves have pinkish blotches

☺ Dryberry, downy mildew.

☺ Spray with BRAVO.

RHUBARB

3 Brown rot at base of plant

☺ Crown rot.

☺ Improve drainage and reduce watering.

Wilting and death of plant

☺ Sclerotinia.

☺ Destroy plants. Sterilise soil with BASAMID. Water evenly over summer.

4 Yellowish spots on leaves with rust-coloured pustules on lower surface

☺ Rust.

☺ Destroy infected leaves. Spray with GARDEN MASTER at first sign of infection.

5 Small brown spots on leaves which go red, brown or black

☺ Leaf spot.

☺ Remove and burn infected leaves. Keep plants growing vigorously with fertiliser and regular watering. Spray with GARDEN MASTER.

1   Angular, light brown patches. Furry growth on underside of leaves

☹   Downy mildew.

☺   Remove and burn infected leaves. Spray with GARDEN MASTER.

STONEFRUIT (APRICOT, CHERRY, NECTARINE, PEACH, PLUM)

2   Leaves emerge deformed and blistered, usually pink or yellow in colour

☹   Leaf curl.

☺   Spray with CHAMPION COPPER, BRAVO or GREENGUARD at bud swelling.

3   Leaves yellowing in spots. Orange or red pustules on undersides of leaves in summer and autumn

☹   Rust.

☺   Spray with BRAVO or FRUIT TREE SPRAY.

4   Small brown spots that dry out and leave clean, round holes. Fruit may have scabs and skin cracks. Gum exudes from twigs

☹   Shot hole.

☺   Spray with BRAVO or FRUIT TREE SPRAY.

5   Fruit develops a brown rot, which spreads quickly through the fruit when it approaches maturity. Trees sometimes exude a gum

☹   Brown rot.

☺   Spray during flowering with BRAVO or GREENGUARD.

6   Leaves turn a silvery grey colour and growth slows

☹   Silver leaf.

☺   Most common in areas with mild, wet winters. Remove and burn infected branches. Prune only on dry days and sterilise secateurs thoroughly. Seal pruning cuts with BACSEAL PRUNING PAINT.

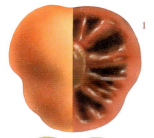

1 Swollen, distorted, empty fruit

☹ Bladder plum

☺ Infected shoots should be removed during growing season. Spray with CHAMPION COPPER at bud swelling.

2 Circular, water-soaked spots with dark centres; margins of large lesions that become raised

☹ Bacterial spot.

☺ Spray with CHAMPION COPPER or FRUIT TREE SPRAY.

3 Distortion and rapid dieback of growing tips. Blackening of stems. Spots or scabs on leaves and fruit. Trees may exude gum

☹ Stone fruit blast.

☺ Actively growing trees are resistant to infection. Prune out infected tissue and spray with CHAMPION COPPER. Spreads rapidly in wet weather.

Insects clustered on young leaves

☹ Aphids.

☺ Spray with NATURE'S WAY INSECT SPRAY, MALDISON or FRUIT TREE SPRAY.

4 Young leaves webbed together and eaten

☹ Leaf roller caterpillar.

☺ Spray with CARBARYL, MALDISON or FRUIT TREE SPRAY.

5 Young growing tips wither and die back. Boring insect found in terminal shoots and in fruit

☹ Oriental fruit moth.

☺ Spray with CARBARYL or FRUIT TREE SPRAY at two to three-week intervals.

6 Leaves eaten and left as transparent skeletons. Black slug-like insects present

☹ Cherry pear slug.

☺ Spray with CARBARYL, FRUIT TREE SPRAY or PYRETHRUM.

1 Leaves yellow (stippled) and dehydrated, particularly in hot, dry weather. Minute insects under leaves

☹ Mites.

☺ Spray with MAVRIK, MITE KILLER or FRUIT TREE SPRAY.

2 Silvering of foliage. Scarring and distortion on fruit skin

☹ Thrips.

☺ Spray with MAVRIK, CONFIDOR or FRUIT TREE SPRAY at flowering.

STRAWBERRY

3 Insects clustered on new leaves, causing foliage distortion

☹ Aphids.

☺ Spray on appearance with MALDISON, PYRETHRUM or NATURE'S WAY INSECT SPRAY.

4 Leaves stippled yellow or rusty brown in colour. Fine webbing and reddish mites on undersides of leaves

☹ Mites.

☺ Most common in hot, dry weather. Spray at first appearance in early spring with MITE KILLER, MAVRIK, GARDEN MASTER or NATURE'S WAY INSECT SPRAY.

Plants cease to thrive and do not crop. Roots diseased and rotting

☹ Verticillium and other soil-borne fungal diseases.

☺ Sterilise soil with BASAMID. Alternatively, grow in containers.

5 Leaves develop brown or black spots

☹ Leaf spot.

☺ More prevalent in humid weather. Water plants when quick drying of leaves and fruit is possible. Pick fruit thoroughly. Spray with BRAVO or CHAMPION COPPER.

1 Fruit develops grey mould and rots

☹ Botrytis, grey mould.

☺ More prevalent in wet weather. Pick off and destroy infected fruit. Spray with BRAVO.

TAMARILLO

2 Holes in leaves

☹ Caterpillars.

☺ Spray with CARBARYL or MAVRIK.

3 Tiny white insects on undersides of leaves which fly when disturbed

☹ Whitefly.

☺ Spray with MAVRIK, TARGET or NATURE'S WAY INSECT SPRAY.

4 White, powdery mould starting in spots and spreading over the leaf. Leaf develops black patches, turns yellow, then drops off

☹ Powdery mildew.

☺ Not difficult to control with fungicides. Spray with GARDEN MASTER or NATURE'S WAY FUNGUS SPRAY early in spring to catch the first infection and then at two to three-week intervals.

INDEX